Copyright © 2015 by Venison E. Nelson
All rights reserved. This book or any portion thereof
may not be reproduced or used in any manner whatsoever
without the express written permission of the publisher
except for the use of brief quotations in a book review.

Printed in the United States of America

First Printing, 2015

ISBN 978-0692475027

Big Red Fire Truck Publishing
1879 Whitworth Drive
Riverdale, GA 30296

www.ignorecowpatties.com

IGNORE COW PATTIES
Venison Nelson

FOREWORD

I want to first thank God, for the being creator of all persons, places, and things; Jesus Christ, for being my Lord and Savior; and the Holy Spirit, for delivering the words of God to me.

I want to thank my mother, Queen. Not only would I not be here without you, but thank you for never giving up on me, always motivating me, and being Momma when I need you. I'm proud of you.

I want to thank the Ol' Lady Lizzie Nelson, my grandmother. Though you have moved on, you picked me up and dusted me off more than I can count. Your belief in me and the faith you gave me cannot be deterred.

To my brother Samuel, thank you for being the big brother to your big brother. I would have fallen many times if it weren't for you.

To my wife Tyesha, I love you so much. Thank you for being by my side no matter how many mountains we climb or valleys we fall.

To my boys Patrick and Jakobie, I'm proud of you. Never give up on God, because he will never give up on you.

To my uncles Carl and Albert, I wouldn't be a man without either of you.

To my Auntie Faye and Mauricia, I'm proud of you. You took on a hard task with the Ol' Lady.

To the rest of my family, I love you. Thank you for loving me, too.

To my friends thank you for being a friend to the true me, Vee.

PREFACE

This book began as a quick fifteen minute read for the soul. I initially wrote only the first chapter. When the words were first delivered, I didn't use the word you will see repeated throughout the book. When in the world, you use worldly words. I did not write this book; I was merely the typist. The story itself is a metaphor. It should be identifiable with several events in anyone's life. It can also be said this is a metaphor of my life. I believe that there is substance to the book, simply because 8 years after writing the first chapter, it renewed my faith. After reading the book, I'm tied and bound to every character. I have, in some form or fashion, shared their journey.

It was 1995, and my uncle and I were working together performing handyman work. We were both between jobs, and although we had been unemployed for some time, we weren't really looking for work; we enjoyed the hustle of surviving. I liked doing handyman jobs because there were no drug tests, I set my own hours, and there was no policy about drinking on the job.

My uncle had a church member who needed us to fix a problem in her bathroom. My uncle stopped by and picked me up. I jumped in the truck, and when he told me that I should make about $100 off this job, I was all smiles. Most of my friends worked for minimum wage, and they had to work 20 hours to make a $100 in a day. He shared with me the sermon his pastor had delivered on Sunday invigorated his spirit. He spoke about his deliverance from the desire to smoke crack cocaine. I listened, and even though this was his 20th or 30th deliverance, I was proud of him. He was like the father I never had. He told me things that he felt a man needed to know. Things like, "A man can build and tear down the world with a knife, a screwdriver, pliers, a crowbar, and hammer, so always keep them. You can also build and tear down your life with them." I hated carrying a wallet, and he fussed about my lack of a wallet by saying, "A wallet is a man's filing cabinet. How you gonna stay organized without a wallet?"

We arrived at the woman's house, which sat in the middle of a poor neighborhood in West End. To me, the house wasn't even worth $100, and I started feeling my profit margin disappearing as we walked up the broken concrete steps to a porch with missing planks of wood. He tapped me on the shoulder. "Look at all that money we can make." I shook my head, thinking that the best thing we could do was help this woman move.

Before we could press the doorbell, we were greeted by 4 little kids. The oldest was probably 9 years old.

"Hey, where's your momma?" my uncle asked.

The door closed, and the oldest yelled at the top of her lungs, "Momma the man that plays guitar at the church is here." He actually played bass, and had done so at the church since he was a teenager.

A big lady in her gown and housecoat came to the door. "Hey Nelson," she said. "Com'on in. Let me show you the bathroom."

The house was as cold as the winter day outside, with a smell of mothballs, bleach, and chicken grease. The floors of the house had the pitches and lumps of an uneven ghetto street, and they creaked and cracked as we walked to the small bathroom at the back of the house. In front of the toilet, there was an old rusted aluminum TV tray lying on the floor with one nail holding it in place.

She said, "Something needs to be done in here. It gets cold when you in the bathroom. The draft comes from under the house, and it is enough to make you run up outta here. That cold gets in my joints and it makes my ankles ache."

My uncle reached down and pulled the tray from the floor as if the nail wasn't there. We could see straight down to the ground. Cold air rushed us like a football team. He asked, "You want a new floor in here?"

She said, "I want a new floor, but I ain't got new floor money. I've got a piece of linoleum that I want to put in there but it doesn't make sense to put it down with the floor like that."

We stepped into the dining room. As my uncle negotiated with the lady on the work to be done, she told him about buying Christmas presents for her children and the cost of her bills. She wasn't getting many hours at work, but God would make a way.

I stopped listening. Whenever God was brought up, money was subtracted off the final cost of labor. I tuned back in when she asked her daughter to get her purse. The lady retrieved a $100 bill and asked if he could get the materials needed with it. He assured her that it would be tight, but he could do it.

We jumped in the truck, and the first stop was the liquor store on the corner. We bought a 12 pack of Bud Ice, then went to the hardware store and spent $60 on supplies. What we did was nothing you'd see on HGTV; we Afro-engineered. We drank beers, and he told me more about his deliverance. I nodded, drank beer after beer, smoked cigarettes, and geared myself up for the work in front of us.

I removed the toilet and sat it on the front porch. We weren't removing the tub, so we had to determine how we would level the old floor with the new floor. It was nothing we hadn't done before. As my uncle supervised, I removed the vanity cabinet and placed it outside the door.

He handed me the crowbar and told me, "Alright, from the tub to the door, all that needs to come out."

Demolition was my thing; I was all over it. I started at the wall behind the toilet. With the first pull, the floor came up and some of the wall came down.

"Goddammit VEE!" he said. "Be careful. We fixing the floor. Don't mess up the walls."

I nodded and went for the second pry. It was the same result. The wall's paneling buckled and begin to crack about 18 inches from the floor.

"Goddammit VEE! Gimme that damn crowbar! You gonna mess up our profit being all flip."

Flip meant "flippant." He always said I rushed doing everything.

My uncle took the crowbar and delicately pried the next board, making sure not to get near the wall. With his pry, the board came up and brought half of a rotted floor joist with it.

"God DAMN!"

Every pull it seems to expose a bigger problem. My uncle began cussing and naming all of his problems; he was mad at his wife, his kids, and the original builder of the house for not using treated wood, even though the house was probably built in 1910, well before treated wood existed. His whole story about deliverance was forgotten.

At that moment, God gave me the original book, which is now the first chapter.

I admit again, I didn't write this book. I typed what was passed to me. It took 18 years to write it. I refused to sit down and put one word on page or screen. None of my friends were writers. I didn't want the burden of answering any questions about it. I didn't want to be looked at as odd by my friends or family. Plus, I didn't want to go through the work to put it out. I wanted to be a rapper, later a software developer, then songwriter, then a business man, but never a book writer.

I was faced with a depressing event 8 years ago when my grandmother was dying. One night, God said, "Get Up!" I woke up and typed the entire first chapter of this book. I also typed my understanding of the metaphors in the book. I gave it to a few of my friends and my mom to read, but that was it.

In 2013, I was faced again with insurmountable odds. I had forgotten writing the book. My mother gave it to me to read for myself, and it truly renewed my faith and belief that God had a plan for me. I decided to retype it, but God had other plans—he added several more chapters. I merely typed what He told me to.

GREEN PASTURES

There was a man whose name isn't important. He was traveling a long, winding road through farmlands in a place that is also not important. During the trip, not one car approached from the direction opposite that of which he was travelling. He saw one or two cars behind him and ahead of him, but they turned their respective ways.

While driving, he was awestruck by the beauty of the landscape. There were flat plains, hills, and occasional mountains made of the greenest grass he had ever seen. He had been driving for quite some time when the car stopped, for a reason that—you guessed it—isn't important.

After several attempts to start the car, he got out of and popped the hood. He pulled the dipstick and removed the oil cap, as if it could remedy the issue of the car stopping. He finally came to terms with the fact that, besides how to put gas in them, all he knew about cars was what he demonstrated at the DMV to get his license. He was certain that a stroll was in his future. He looked in the direction he came from and thought to himself, *It must have been 20 odd miles since I passed a gas station. Not to mention the last thing I want to do is go backwards.*

He looked in the direction he was heading and he saw the long, winding road disappear into the hills and grassy plains. He could see what looked to be a sign across a flat plain with very low hills in the far distance. He couldn't read it, but he convinced himself it was a gas station sign. He was reluctant at first but it appeared he needed to cross the pasture to get to the sign.

He decided to give it a go and approached the fence surrounding the pasture. He climbed the fence, placed his jacket over the barbed wire, and carefully lifted himself up and over. He began walking as soon as his feet hit the ground.

When he first started he was saying to himself, "This could be worse. I'm lucky. I'm in good health and I can walk this with my legs tied behind my back. It's one of the nicest days I can remember. This is the nicest, greenest—CRAP!"

In the middle of a pasture he stepped in cow crap.

"Crap!" he yelled again. He tried to shake the mess off of his shoe. The scent was unmistakable. While kicking and wiping his foot in the grass, an event occurred that Confucius described best: "If one shoe crappy, the other shoe is too crappy."

He stepped in another cow patty with the other foot.

"CRAP!" he screamed. He suddenly forgot about the nice day, his great health, and the beauty of the landscape. All he could think about was the mess on his best shoes.

He started lamenting over the crap—the crap smell, the crap possession. He became crap-focused. He was crap-aware; crap-conscious, even. He became overly mindful of the piles around him as he progressed through the pasture. He stopped every 10 to 20 steps to survey the crap that lie before him. If there was crap in the vicinity, he would alter his course to circumvent the crap. In some areas, the grass was higher than others, making it not as easy to see. He wasn't paying attention to the grass blade height/crap visibility ratio; he made a few more missteps.

"CRAP! CCRAPP!! CCCRAPPP!!!"

His shoes were loaded with crap. His mind was raced, trying to find someone other than himself to blame for his turmoil. He was stuck in a crap waltz, and the crap refused to let him lead. He was angry with the cows, the farmer, the car manufacturer, his mechanic, his landlord, and his 9th grade biology teacher.

He needed a crap deterrent, or, at the very least, a way around all of the crap. The answer hit him,

He made a 45-degree bee line for the fence, avoiding crap wherever it lay. The crap was sparse near the fence, but there was still crap. While attempting to avoid it, he would get too close to the fence. The first time, he tore his pants on the barbed wire. The second time, the fence drew blood.

"Great," he said to himself. "Now I need a tetanus shot. No telling what else has touched that fence."

H suddenly caught himself about to step in another bovine gift. He moved his foot and stepped on a loose, smooth, seemingly out of place rock. He began falling backward, but he never hit the ground. Instead, the barbed wire fence caught him. He screamed in agony as the barbs dug into his back and scratched his arms, hands, and side.

As if he were a ninja from a Kung Fu movie, he sprung from the fence. The pain was excruciating. The deepest punctures were in the middle of his back where he couldn't see or reach. He could feel the blood as it soaked his shirt. He thought of the scars that would be left behind, the horrible disfigurement, and the high dose of poison must have been flowing through his body from the multiple punctures from the fence. Tetanus, in his mind, had turned into H1N1, Ebola, Avian Flu, Staph infection, Mad Cow, Hoof and Mouth, and countless other bacteria, diseases, and viruses.

He continued to walk. He continued following the fence but played it safe by leaving more distance between the fence and him. Still crap-aware, he stopped every ten steps to survey the amount of crap in the path. While observing the crap-density along his path, over near the middle of the field he saw something he couldn't believe. He said to himself, "I've got to see this for myself. I got to make sure my eyes aren't deceiving me."

He walked over to the object that had distracted him, and when he found that it was exactly what he thought it was. It was THE BIGGEST CRAP he's ever seen.

"Wow! Do you see this crap?" he yelled.

He stood there in amazement at the massive crap. He was slightly amused. To make sure it was crap, he found a stick in the pasture and poked the outer surface of the crap; he had to stir up the crap to accept the crap he had encountered. When the pungent odor hit his nose, he said, "Yep, just as I thought. CRAP!"

Because of the scent that had filled the air, he began to walk faster. He was behooved to realize that his past focal point of marvel wasn't the biggest crap; there were more piles that were just as big, if not bigger. Each time he would stop and yell, "Do you see this crap?"

There was no one there to acknowledge or respond, but he felt it was his duty to take time and express the fact that, while in a cow pasture, he was seeing crap. This went on for quite some time until he realized the day was starting to get away from him. He went back to the fence to continue his journey.

While near the fence, he looked at the other pasture. The grass wasn't as green as it was in the pasture where he walked. And he thought, *They say that the grass is always greener on the other side. The pasture over there isn't as green as the pasture I'm in. I've learned from my experience in this pasture where the grass is green the crap is plentiful, so that must mean there is less crap in the other pasture.*

His crap-woes were about to be over. He crossed into the other pasture and began to hike in the direction he was headed. At first, he was happy to step confidently on the hardened dirt area near the fence. Then he stepped onto an area that appeared to be a dirt mound, as gravity and inertia worked together, his foot broke through the dry crusted top of… you guessed it. Crap. The most repugnant odor yet flooded the air.

"CCCRRRAAPPP! Do you see this CRAP? It can't get any worse that this! I can't escape crap no matter where I go or what I do!"

He stomped and kicked as if he had stepped in the meanest bed of fire ants. Then reality set in. Though there wasn't as much green grass, it was a cow pasture; there was still going to be crap, possibly more crap than the last pasture. He found a flaw in his logic of changing pastures: where green grass meant the absence of grazing cows, the absence of grass surely meant cows had been there.

He began to question all of his decisions. Panic set in. He thought of every problem that he had ever had. He thought of the current situation. Then, he thought of the daylight disappearing. He first picked up the pace, and then began to jog, then run. He said to himself, "Ignore cow patties!"

He began sloshing through crap, not concerned

with the consequences. It flew everywhere. His shoes were, at this point, ready to be throw away. His pants were covered in crap up to the knees. In his heated sprint, he had become so covered in crap that its weight became a burden, slowing his pace and making him lethargic. He made a step, lost traction, and began slipping. He could feel himself being propelled forward and fell face first into crap. He sprung up and, without daring to open his mouth, yelled, "MMMMMMMM!"

He used his hands to wipe the crap from his eyes. He took off his jacket and shirt to use them to wipe away as much crap as he could. He reviewed the blood stains from the fiasco against the fence. Some were small streaks from scratches, others were small drops. There were three spots that were about the size of the palm of his hand, and he could see where blood ran down from those punctures. Those were the ones he had the most concern for. He could feel them with every step, as if they continued to open more as he walked.

His frustration at its highest level, he screamed out, "I can't believe this CRAP!"

Frustrated and feeling as if he had been transported to his own personal purgatory, he suddenly realized he couldn't see the sign. It was the first he had turned his attention away from the crap long enough to notice how far off course he was. He looked in all directions, and the sign was nowhere to be found.

"Oh Crap." he said sighed. "This has to be the crappiest day of my life."

He realized following the fence and changing pastures had taken him completely off of course. As he looked back, he noticed that the fence bent and turned like the Mississippi River. The other pasture was nowhere near in the direction he originally embarked.

He crossed back into the green pasture and walked until he was in the middle of the pasture and the greenest part. Crap wise, he was in the proverbial situation of being "knee deep in it."

The course correction worked, and the sign was back in perspective. He had so much time trying to dodge crap, stopping in awe of crap, stirring up crap, running through crap, falling in crap, and finding out that—no matter the pasture—there will be crap, that he had lost track of his original objective.

Quickening his pace to make up for all of the

wasted time, he began getting close enough to the sign to read it. What it said is not important, but at the base of the sign there was a metal building that stretched as far as the eye could see. He walked as fast as he could, but it seemed as if the building was moving. The walk became more laborious with every step. Once he got close enough to see the details of the building—where it had rusted, where it appeared repairs had been made—he saw a door. He ran to the fence, threw his crap covered jacket on the barbs, and hopped it easily. He ran to the door and began first knocking, then beating on it as he yelled, "Hello, Hello! I'm out here! Help! I need Help!"

With no answers to his calls, he began to believe all sorts of things. *There is no one to help*, he thought. *I probably can't find my way back to the car. My car has probably been stolen. I can't walk another step. I'm thirsty. I'm hungry. What if something happens and nobody finds me? What if these cuts and scratches go septic and there is no one that will find me? What if I DIE! Who would care!*

He felt as if he didn't have a family member, friend, or acquaintance. He began walking to the closest end of the building. With every step, he felt dread. The wounds in his back burned from sweat, but he was convinced that it was from the coalitions of viruses and bacteria invading his body. He drug his feet desperately, as if he had been walking across Death Valley and the end of the building was an oasis.

Reaching the end of the building he saw remnants of civilization. There was a smoking pit, where the employees would congregate and smoke cigarettes. He saw a group of people head into the smoking pit. He ran to them and said,"Boy, are you guys a sight for sore eyes! My car broke down across the pasture, and I need a gas station and a mechanic, or at least a way to make a phone call. I'm thirsty, I'm filthy, and I need a doctor, because of these cuts in my back. I didn't think I was going to make it. That pasture had crap everywhere!"

The men stood there with a blank stare, marveling at him as if he were a talking statue—a talking statue made of crap. He was covered from head to toe. His clothing was stained and clumped. It was on his face, hands, and feet. As everyone else stared with looks of amazement, fear, disappointment, or just plain awe of his image, a thin fellow with flaxen hair and a scruffy beard, wearing dirty coveralls and a skull cap, spoke for the group.

"Man, you look like crap, you're covered in crap, and you smell like crap."

The traveler responded, "I know! That's what I just said. I need help. I gotta get this crap off of me."

The man responded, "Well I ain't touching you, and you're nasty to be out there rolling in crap. Looks like you were so full of crap you exploded!"

Slowly their faces turned to smirks, sneers, and flat out laugh in your face expressions. Some shook their heads in disbelief. The man had just what he wanted: an audience. What followed was a monologue fit for the greatest in late night television host. Using the same words, the traveler had previously used. The man continued on with a cigarette in his mouth, an ash the length of half the cigarette bouncing merrily up and down as if it was performing an acrobatic feat from the circus.

The man said, "This the biggest pile of crap I've ever seen. Do you see this crap? I mean, really, do you see this crap? I've never seen this much crap in my life." He walked around him, yelling, "Boy do you stink. What fragrance are you wearing? Crappe Cologne? I mean, I really don't believe this crap. It ain't one place on you where there ain't no crap. You even got crap in your eyes. I'm sure that gives you a very crappy outlook on life.

Look at his ears. He probably can't hear crap. You got a crap mustache, crap beard, you look like Santa Crap. You look like an educated man, wearing your crap and gown. Looks like you were standing dead center and didn't move when the crap hit the fan. Let me guess, right here, right now, this got to be the crappiest day of your life. I bet he's the latest employee they just hired here. He's probably management. Boy your momma must be proud of the dump she gave to the earth."

With every single zinger the man threw, there were several people encouraging him to keep going. They pointed, laughed, and made their own personal comments. Others turned their heads and ignored the shenanigans, making it perfectly understood they didn't want to be involved.

The traveler stood there and took the onslaught of jokes. He was embarrassed, and his sagging shoulders, low hanging head, and expression of self-disappointment let it be known. He thought of all the sayings he said previously that the man was repeating, and how it was now fodder. At the time he said them, they were true expressions of how he felt. He wondered how anxious he would be to help someone in his plight if he was standing in the crowd instead of in front of it. He wondered if he would laugh and add to the destruction of the person. But the statement about his mother brought him back to life. He had taken all that he could.

He spoke with great authority in his voice and said "That's enough! All I need—"

Before he could finish, the local comedian said, "I don't wanna hear that crap!" The only thing that was missing was a drummer in a cheap tuxedo giving a drum hit of BA-dum-bum-dum, followed by a cymbal crash. The traveler's pride was destroyed, and he slumped even further.

He pointed at the fellow throwing jabs as he said, "All I need is directions to a gas station and a phone. THAT'S ALL I NEED."

In his embarrassment, he didn't that care he was covered in crap, so he didn't ask for a way to clean up. He forgot his thirst. Medical attention was unimportant. There was no way he was asking anyone for a ride; he wouldn't offer one if the shoe was on the other foot and his antagonist was standing there covered in crap. With his torn pride on the offensive he added, "PLEASE, THAT'S ALL I NEED."

The man, now appearing to either be afraid of him or sympathetic to his plight, said, "Yeah, go back across the pasture the same way you came. He pointed in the original direction the traveler was heading. "When you get to the road, walk up the hill. When you get to the top of the hill, you'll see there is a gas station with a mechanic, phone booth, hotel, and hospital all right there together."

WALKING BLINDLY THROUGH THE FAMILIAR

The traveler looked at the man and said, "Thank you." He rolled his eyes as he turned and walked off with a posture that read don't touch me, as if anyone would touch him in his current condition. He walked down the side of the building, exhausted and with no plan.

He had no idea where his car was in relation to the building, or where he had crossed out of the pasture. The building was long with rusted doors every football stadium length. He didn't count the doors when he was walking, as he was sure he would find salvation at the building. He could see his previous footsteps and started to remember the patterns of rust and the machinery attached to the building. The sun was low in the sky; it was no way he would be able to cross the pasture before dark. He took a deep breath and kept walking. Determined to identify something in the rust patches of the building, he came to a point that looked familiar. There were no footprints ahead. He went to the fence and, like he had done three times already, he placed his jacket on the barbed wire and crossed back into the pasture.

He walked along with his head down, not because he was looking for cow patties, but because he felt sorry for himself. He was trying to determine how he got into this situation. His pace altered, dependent on how much thought he was placing into the current situation. No longer did he care about stepping in the patties. The crap didn't matter; he just wanted out of the pasture.

As he came to the top of a hill, he marveled at the beautiful sunset. It brought a renewed strength as well as fear. Soon it would be pitch black dark. He knew that he wouldn't make it out of the pasture before sunset; he doubted he would make it half way before it was too dark. He couldn't run anymore. Physically and mentally, he just couldn't do it, and the results yielded the first time also encouraged him not to run..

As the sun set, the temperature dropped and the wind picked up speed, adding a cold briskness to the air. It didn't matter how cold it was. He had to keep moving. His shirt was soaked with sweat, blood, and crap. His jacket was heavy. He buttoned it and continued to walk. Soon, he couldn't see his hand in front of him. He took shorter steps and continued on through the valley and hills. He saw the last glimmer of the waning sunset and another large hill ahead of him. He could hear the cicadas, crickets, other insects, and animals joining in on nature's symphony. He shuffled his feet as he walked to avoid stepping into a mole hole. While he wasn't sure that moles lived in the area, it could definitely yield bad results; a sprained or twisted ankle would make the trip across the pasture almost impossible.

It seemed that he wasn't stepping in as much crap as before, but he was still encountering it. He would kick it sometimes, as he attempted to navigate the land with limited light. He stopped yelling at the crap and let go of his frustration. He and the crap had begun a relationship.

The grass appeared to be higher as he walked across the valley. The earth under his feet was soft and mostly mud. He continued picking up more weight. He found himself thinking about his childhood days spent playing in the mud with his friends. The sun had provided heat and cooling effects to the mud as they tackled each other. This was hardly the feeling he was experiencing. He smiled, shook his head, and quoted *The Wizard of Oz* to himself, "We're not in Kansas anymore."

The more he walked, the sound of cicadas and crickets was drowned out by the sound of frogs. He stumbled over a large limb that was at least 5 feet long and completely out of place. He couldn't remember seeing one tree during his initial crossing of the cow pasture; all he remembered was crap. He picked up the stick and used it as a walking stick. It gave him the ability to test the softness of the wet earth in front of him.

As he walked forward, he could see eyes reflecting moonlight. Well this was concerning, he knew nothing about wild life of the area. At first he thought it was frogs, but as he got closer and closer he started believing it was snakes. He stopped and began contemplating going around the area where he saw the eyes that appeared to be stalking him. The grunts around him were getting closer, and he thought, "Wolves! What if they have me surrounded? At least I have this stick." He began practicing his offensive and defensive skills with the stick. Like the old cartoons, he parried, dodged, thrusted, spun, and BAM! He struck himself right between the eyes with the stick. He covered the bridge of nose with his hand and yelled silently to himself not to give his location to the wolves. He was scared that soon blood would start flowing from his nose and provide a scent that could be tracked. The throbbing pain came in waves. As soon as he believed he had gained his composure, the pain would return. He could feel the area swelling, and his frustration and fear grew with it.

Now that he was convinced he was being stalked by both man-eating vipers and wolves, he felt it wasn't safe to stay in the area. He assumed he was probably in the middle of the valley. He really needed to make it to the hill. He felt he would be safer on the hill and able to watch for any predators that may come for him. He forgot that running hadn't worked well for him in his first try and threw caution to the wind. He began jogging through the deep mud. The further he jogged, the wetter, colder, and heavier the mud became. He made a great leap and his leg sunk into the moist ground almost to the knee. He thought to himself, *What if this is like quicksand? What if I began sinking, will anyone ever find me?*

He started counting the family and friends that would miss him. How would they know to check this area? He began to realize that leaving the road had been a terrible idea.

As he came to that realization, he heard a grunt, "RRRRRRRUUUUHHHH, GRRRRRRRUUUUUUUUNNNNHHHH." The moment of attack was upon him, and that was obviously the attack call of the wolves and snakes. He swung the stick wildly leaping from one plunge in the mud to another. His heart was racing, and he was certain the wolves and snakes were about to strike at any time. With a great leap, he felt himself sink waist deep into the soft earth, and he came face to face with a pair of eyes.

He was paralyzed. The sound came once more, "RRRRUUUUHHHH, GGGGRRRRUUUNNNNHHHH," and as quickly as they had appeared in front of him, they were gone.

He used the stick to pull himself from the murky, muddy depths. As he pulled, he felt a large, cold stone beside him. With the stick in his right hand and his left hand pressing on the stone he freed himself. He laid flat across the mud to spread his weight and he used the stick to survey for other stones in front of him. Actually he was using the stick to ward off any snakes, and wolves that was about to launch a frontal assault. When his stick would strike one of the large rocks, he made his way to it and used it to help keep himself above the marshland.

"GGGRRRRRUUUNNNHHH, GGGRRRUUUUNNNHHHH."

He stopped and looked to his left. He could see those piercing eyes, but this time he could make out the shape of a frog as it hopped forward, its landing met with a shallow splash.

He took a deep breath and closed his eyes. He listened and heard a small trickle of water in front of him. He continued to drag himself across the area that he now recognized as a small stream that was slowly drying up. Soon, he could feel the cool running water under his feet, and the ground beneath him became rockier. When he reached the deepest part of the stream, the moonlight glistened off of the surface of the water. The water was above his ankles. He washed his hands, and then he grabbed handfuls of water and washed his face. As the water washed the crap from his face, a feeling of peace to come over him. He continued on his journey.

When he reached the other side of the stream, he was met with an almost vertical climb to the hill before him. He walked towards the direction of the town until he found an area that appeared to be easier to cross. As he trekked up the incline, he could see lights of passing cars coming from the highway in the distance. He told himself, *I've got a long way to go.*

His clothes were now soaked with both water and crap. The wind blowing was making him exhausted and miserable, but he kept climbing. The hill felt more like a mountain as he made his way up the steep slope. He could hear cows mooing and grunting. He kept stepping until he reached a plateau of the hill. He stopped and observed the stars. He could see man-made lights of civilization in the distance. Every once and a while, he saw what appeared to be a shooting star; in reality it was just a car making its way down the highway.

He sat down to rest and catch his breath for the walk down the hill. Everything around him seemed quiet. He leaned back in the grass and placed his hands over his head. The wind made a whistling sound as it passed through the blades of grass. He found peace in the silence and breathed deeply. His will to go on was fading with every moment. He thought of just lying there until the morning in his misery. With his eyes closed, he thought of the path he was on and the possible outcome if he would have just kept walking. He blamed himself for being the master of making the wrong decisions.

He thought of a time once before, when he found an item on the internet he just swore he had to have. He was remodeling and had priced a similar item at a high end store he loved to frequent. He had to settle on an item with less features because the cost of what he wanted was astronomical. He was still saving money to get the one that was of lesser value. The price of the item was too good to be true; it was equal to the amount of the item he was saving to purchase. He had to have it.

He had already done the work to get the item to

fit. He had taken all of the measurements and done extensive research on the quality, the look, and the added features of the item. He couldn't wait to show it off. Throwing caution to the wind, he decided to act on the deal of a lifetime. He emailed the seller and was promptly returned a phone number to call. He called the seller who was more than knowledgeable about the product. It was like he was an expert able to tell him everything that he had read about the product verbatim.

The seller told him if he couldn't find a buyer, he was going to keep it for himself. When it came to time to talk money, the seller lowered the price even more to motivate him to buy it. He explained that he'd rather sell it than have it sit in the warehouse and get damaged by workers with the grace of a bull in a china shop. The seller told him that he would have it on a truck headed his way first thing in the morning, and if he would send him the payment via Western Union that night, That was music to his ears. He could send the payment that night; there was a Western Union not 5 minute walk from his place. He retrieved the information from the seller, and as soon as he hung up the phone he went straight to the Western Union, paid for the item, and paid an additional fee to complete the transaction with his credit card The vendor gave him a confirmation number and advised him to give the correct control number to the recipient so he would be able to get the payment with no problems.

Using the email address he used to initially contact the seller, he sent the control number. The seller replied,

Dear Sir:
Thank you for your business. As soon as I have the money in hand I will return an email with the time and date of delivery. You will be very happy with your new item.
Thanks.

He remembered sitting that night imagining all of the praises and accolades he would receive once it was installed and he could show it off. He also remembered waiting for an email that never came. The next morning, he called the seller's number; there was no answer. He went to the website of the trucking agency that the seller claimed to represent and found the business's number. Upon reaching the operator, he demanded to speak to the seller. The operator promptly told him there was no one there by that name. His heart throbbed in his throat. He told the receptionist the model and serial number of the item that was to be shipped to him. She told him they neither the item, nor a warehouse in which to store it.

He went back to the website where he located the item and he clicked on the link that took him to the site of the trucking company. This time he noticed the website address was completely different from the actual website of the transit company. He called Western Union. They told him there was nothing they could do. If the seller had the correct confirmation number, he was authorized to pick up the money.

He called the transit company back and demanded to speak to the owner. The receptionist let him down even further when she explained that the company consisted of her, her husband, and son. The position the seller claimed to have didn't even exist in their company. She apologized and explained it was a scam. He called the police, who took a report but told him honestly that they had seen this same scam before, and he didn't have a leg to stand on. They warned him of the dangers of transacting business for items unseen. As a caveat, he had lost a whole day of work trying to get to the bottom of the scam. His boss was very angry because it ended up costing him a lot of money, too.

He thought of several other instances of bad decisions that plagued his past, but then came to the conclusion that it didn't matter. It didn't matter one bit, because he didn't just keep the path he decided to walk across THIS pasture. Now the only thing that mattered was walking back to the lighted area he could see from the top of the hill. He breathed in deeply and exhaled each time with a sigh.

He was so exhausted, and he knew he had further to go. Though it was a long way, he knew what he had to do. He sat up and attempted to survey the lay of the land to plan the best route, but the lack of immediate light made it difficult to discern. Once again, he felt he was over-burdened with crap and needed to rest more. He leaned back against the grass again, closed his eyes, and shook his head one time after another as the thoughts of his day raced through his mind.

As he lay on the hill, he heard a crunching noise behind him. CRUNCH! CRUNCH! He leaned forward looking to see if he could see anything, but there was nothing there. He leaned back and surrendered to waiting until the morning to move again. He was sure his car was gone and everyone he'd encounter would be like the guy who gave him directions. He preferred not to deal with anymore that day. All of a sudden there it was again, CRUNCH, CRUNCH. And then it sped up CRUNCH, CRUNCH, CRUNCH CRUNCH, and then something really big rumbled under the ground beneath him.

This was cause for action. He grabbed his stick and jumped to his feet, ready to meet the wolves that had been circling him. He swept the grass with the stick just in case it was a pack of ravenous snakes with beady little eyes. He slowly started backing down the hill in the direction of town, glancing over his shoulder and waiting for impending doom. He stopped, patiently waiting for something to move, a flicker of light, or another sound. He kept backing down the hill, sweeping the stick from left to right, when all of a sudden, right next to him, he met the adversary face to face. A roar broke out from the great beast: "MMMMMOOOOOOO" The predatory bovine leaped to all fours and began running, the man was in a full sprint down the hill. He screamed like a mesa-soprano with arachnophobia in a pit full of spiders.

Running like an Appaloosa in the Kentucky Downs, he flew down. He knew there was no threat, but he still felt compelled to continue to run until he suddenly lost traction. There was no crap. It was simply the laws of physics; a biped, running, generating high inertia, with low balance on an incline just doesn't yield positive results. Unaware of how steep the terrain had become, there was no way he could keep up the speed he was running. He dropped his walking stick and began tumbling, shrieking, "CRAP!!!!"

His tumble was like a dry towel in the dryer. He bounced and then seemed to spin in mid-air. He attempted to correct himself on several occasions, which resulted in him just rolling down the hill. Soon he came to a rest at the bottom of the hill. He rolled over onto his back and looked up in the night sky.

"Really? Really? All of this crap in one day? All I wanted to do is just lay here. WHAT DID I DO TO DESERVE THIS!!!!" he screamed at the top of his lungs. "My car broke down, my shoes are screwed, I fell on a barbed wire fence, fell face first in crap, got insulted by the king of all jerks, only to hear I've got to go back the way I came. I almost drowned in mud and got attacked by a mad cow. WHAT ELSE? WHAT ELSE COULD IT BE?"

Another wise word from Confucius: "Ask and you will be answered."

Though they were confused about a moving cow patty invading their space, the fire ants were persistent. They search and searched until they found soft warm flesh and begin biting. He jumped to his feet and began the oddest moonlit 2-step ever. With every chomp he stomped, and he swung at the invisible enemy at the bottom of his pant leg. Balanced on one foot, he swung and beat his pant leg, yelling, "Crap, crap, crap, crap, crap!"

After about the 8th or 9th bite, he didn't feel any more ants moving under his pant leg. He slowed the tempo of his two-step until he tired. When he stopped, he realized he was close enough to the road that he could hear the passing cars and trucks. He began moving quickly toward it, trying to determine how far was he from the lights he had seen. How far was he from his car?

Though he was still a fair distance from the road, he was anxious to make it to a phone. Every once and a while, he would feel a sudden bite from a wayward ant. The weary traveler pressed on until he came face to face with the barbed wire fence that he initially crossed.

THE ROAD AHEAD

Back on the road, he felt more confident that soon he would be able to put some of this day behind him. He began walking toward the lights of the town ahead. He attempted to judge the distance and assumed it was about 4 to 5 miles. He walked like a 4th grader ready to tell on his big brother for breaking fine china.

As he walked, cars whizzed past him, making the temperature more brisk than usual. He wondered what he was going to do when he got to the hotel. He could almost feel the hot shower running down his face, back and chest, washing away the crap. As he imagined the rinse of hot water, an 18-wheeler passed. The wind was punishing and destroyed the vision of the hot shower. He buttoned his jacket, placed his hands in the pockets, and removed clumps of grass, crap and other foreign objects. He left them on the road.

As the cars passed by, he wondered where they were heading. He laughed at the thought of someone stopping and offering him a ride, imagining that the person would morph into the comedian he encountered at the building. "I'd give you a ride but you look like and smell like crap."

He kept walking along the winding road. Each step was starting to take its toll. He could feel his calf muscles begin to tighten. He was sore from his tumble, and the wounds on his back were burning from the sweat and constant movement. He rubbed his brow and felt the knot left by his in ability to handle his now abandoned companion stick like a true ninja warrior. He was so tired and just wanted a drink of water—or maybe something stronger—and to put this day behind him.

He began organizing the steps he needed to take once he reached town. He thought about making a dramatic entrance into the gas station, but he couldn't decide if he should say, "Help!" or "Water!" as he collapsed to the floor. He revised the script several times and finally settled on dropping to one knee in front of the first person he came upon, taking three deep breaths, and begging, "Can you help me please?"

The closer he came to the distant lights it seemed there were nothing but the big 18 wheelers on the road. They would sometimes pass in threes. The wind was brutal. He would turn his back to them to attempt to shield the cold that projected from the trucks.

As he walked along, he saw several things along

the road. It was mostly litter. He saw drink cans that made him long for a drink. He thought of a funny moment from his past. He remembered the advertisements for Coca-Cola. He would quote the advertisement, telling his mother that he had to have, "New Coke, It's The Real Thing!" In the early 80s, the company made the decision to change the formula of Coke to contend with competitor cola Pepsi, whose popularity was slowly increasing. His mother couldn't stand the latest incarnation of high fructose corn syrup and caramel flavoring from Coca-Cola. She stopped buying Coke altogether when the formula changed. It was a treat to have Coke every once and a while, but to just go cold turkey on sugar and caffeine was just selfish in his opinion. His mother said, "That stuff doesn't taste right. They don't know what that crap might do to us over time. I don't like it."

During the post original formula Coca-Cola days, his mom wasn't the same. She seemed to always be grumpy. She began saying that the formula of Coke had changed in the late 60s, and again a few months before the introduction of New Coke. Dropping the modified original formula was the last straw. She swore it was a conspiracy to take away all things that were good in the world. She stockpiled the original Coca-Cola by the bottles on the back porch. Before the change, they only drink Coca-Cola twice a week. When the product was scarce, his mother drank 4 to 6 Cokes a day, and the family had Coke every night for dinner. After there was no more original formula Coke left, his mother was on edge and wiry. She drank coffee in the morning, but during the afternoon and evening she had her caffeine boost with Coke. She moved to ginger ale that had no caffeine. It made the perky bottle rocket personality of his mom the result of a dud; the fuse would light, burned until it went inside the tube, and a couple of sparks came out, but no lift off or pop.

There was no way she would drink the competitors' product. It was all part of the New World Order; Coke and Pepsi would merge and it would be the only cola product. His mother believed that this cola conspiracy would soon turn to cola communism.

One day, he walked in the door and it was like old times. His mom was smiling. She said that the drink manufacturer had come to their senses. It was announced as if it were breaking news during her favorite soap opera, Coca-Cola Classic was supposed to hit the shelves any day. She and her friends planned strategic store visits until someone hit the jackpot finding the precious "Real Thing."

    A few months later, he remembered being

inside of a grocery store with a taste test kiosk. In a blindfolded test, his mom picked New Coke over the Coca-Cola Classic. How ironic.

He snickered to himself and began singing the Coke commercial theme, "It's the real thing... IT'S THE REE-AAL THING—"

VROOM! He was back to reality as another truck passed. As he looked back, it appeared 18 wheelers were coming rhythmically every 10 seconds. As the trucks passed, he turned his back and stepped further away from the road, holding his collar to muffle the noise and the cold. He would take three steps and VROOM! He began looking like a member of a weird ballroom dance duo with his choreographed approach to avoiding the wicked wind.

Suddenly, he had an epiphany: *If I cross to the other side of the road where there are less trucks, and the wind won't be as brutal.*

He thought about it for a minute, and then said to himself, "Wait a minute. Astounding ideas like that are the reason I'm here right now. I'm gonna stay the path."

VROOM! He came to an area of the road where the fence was so close to road that he was walking on the asphalt of the busy highway. VROOM! Then the next VROOM! It was taking him too long to reset in his ritual, instead of three steps between cars, he was only able to take one. As he walked, he passed a large pothole filled with water. Another truck barreled by, splashing the contents of the pothole onto the traveler, he yelled "CRAP!" as the cold, dirty water added to his misery. Then, he felt a familiar splat as he plowed into a cow patty on the side of the road.

This almost made him lose his mind. He grabbed his collar, pulled his jacket up to shield his face, and began charging towards the town. VRROOM! VROOM! VVVRRROOOMMM! The last one was close enough to rip the hairs from his knuckles as it passed. Though he didn't consider it, walking with traffic instead of against it, along with his black jacket, made it very difficult for drivers to see him. The last truck made him consider that maybe the other side of the highway wasn't such a bad idea.

He waited for the last mix of cars and trucks to pass. He was walking downhill, and the precipice of the hill blocked his ability to see when the next accomplice to the wind attack would come. He began to count on the artificial light bouncing off of the hill for a sense of the distance of the next vehicle. He assumed if he saw no headlights, there were no cars, so he walked across the highway to the other side.

With confidence he began walking on the other side of the road, mostly on the hard asphalt. With tense muscles, the walk was more of a waddle. The town seemed to be so far away. The hill he was going down was headed into a deep valley. The traffic slowed as time passed, and soon the lights of the town were gone. His opportunity to survey the land in front of him was available only when a car would pass. Once again, he could hear the musical stylings of cicadas, crickets, and frogs. Along with those sounds, he also heard rushing water—lots of water. He thought of being able to stop and take a drink. Oh, how he wished for water! Within a few more steps he could feel water falling from above. First, it was tiny droplets of mist, and then drop, drop, drop.

"No, NOOOOOOO, not rain!" he said. "CRAP!"

He began to briskly waddle, as he knew what was coming. It was already cold, and in the valley the wind was double the strength of the plateaus or the hills. Big drop, big drop, drizzle; he was again about to get exactly what he asked for. Within fifteen minutes, the drizzle had become a downpour, and the temperature dropped even further.

He walked for another 15 minutes or so until he reached the basin of the valley. Suddenly, he saw something that he hadn't seen in a very long time. Not since he was driving did he see a vehicle coming from the town he was so anxious to reach. He looked as the headlights approach and the windshield wipers swung water from left to right. Not only was this car coming from the opposite direction, but it was slowing down. The car came to a complete stop 20 feet in front of him, and the window came down.

"Hey there buddy need a lift?"

The driver looked like he could star in any horror movie or suspense thriller where people suddenly go missing. He had sparse gray hair and seemed to be too tall for the car he was driving. He appeared to be sweating. and alcohol and the scent of wet dog reeked from the interior of the car.

The traveler responded, "Would you mind taking me to the town ahead? My car broke down and I've been walking for an awful long time."

The driver emphatically shook his head, and said, "I will take you to town in the direction I'm going, but you couldn't pay me to go back that way. My wife left me, my dog ran away, and I lost my job. There's nowhere for a man to get a decent drink. The whole town is a bunch of mixed nuts. Plus, if you need a mechanic, I hear the mechanic up here is much better than the mechanics back there."

The traveler thought about everything that had happened through the day and night. He considered getting in the car and ignoring the cow patties he had all over him. Once he sat in the driver's passenger seat, the seat would be ruined. He knew it wouldn't take long for the driver to realize he was covered in crap.

He looked at the driver and said, "I wish I could take your offer, but I'm covered head to toe in crap, and I'd hate to destroy your seat. I appreciate your offer, though. About how long of a walk do I have before I reach the gas station?"

The driver said, "I'd welcome the companionship, and you're right. You smell like crap. But it's your walk, not mine. You got your mind made up. You got about another mile or two. But you better hurry; the whole town rolls up the sidewalks pretty early."

With that, the driver pulled off, spinning tires and throwing mud and debris. The traveler kept walking. *What if I made the wrong decision?* he thought. He would have welcomed the companionship, also—someone to talk to about this fiasco of a day, someone to listen to and share stories with. He watched as the car's red rear lights disappeared into the rain-soaked distance, and then continued to walk.

Heading toward town, a rusted pick-up truck flew past him. The brake lights came on and lit up the sky ahead. The truck stopped as if it were waiting for him. He approached cautiously as the driver window lowered.

The driver said, "I remember you from the smoke pit earlier. Boy, you been walking! Jump in the back and I'll take you on into town."

The driver had one of those faces that always seemed to be smirking or smiling. Classic rock and the smell of soot poured from inside the cab. He looked clean and refreshed, and his brunette hair was neatly combed to the back. A cooler presumably used as a lunch box sat on the passenger seat.

With a hearty thank you, the traveler climbed on the bumper, over the tailgate, and fell into the back of the truck. He slid his tired body close to the cab. The back of the truck was riddled with beer cans, scrap pieces of wood and metal, a gas can, and fishing tackle.

While driving along the back window slid open and the driver said, "That ole boy had quite the laugh at your expense. Like he can talk. I must admit, I felt bad for ya, but you never asked me for help. But then I guess the neighborly thing would have been to offer help, and for that I'm sorry. You wanna drink?

With eyes of luster like a child on Christmas day he replied, "Yes!" The driver reached into his cooler, pulled out an ice cold can of Coca-Cola Classic, and passed it to him. He cracked the top and almost swallowed the can. It was so refreshing and rewarding after the day he had.

The truck topped the hill and came to a stop with lights blaring in all directions at the gas station. The driver yelled, "Buddy, I hope this will help. I hope you make it where yer headin'. When you take a shower it will all be over. Get that crap off of ya and you'll feel just right"

The traveler thanked him for the ride and the Coke. He jumped off of the back of the truck and walked to the payphone.

THE GAS STATION

Lights lit the gas station as bright as an operating room. There were people moving back and forth as they made their purchases. He watched as the truck pulled off. It backfired, and a big cloud of black smoke blew from the exhaust and clouded around him. He coughed as the noxious gases entered his lungs. He looked at the store and saw 3 people waiting in line to use the only payphone.

A tall, slim, pale man was using the payphone with a solemn look on his face. He seemed out of place in the midst of obvious locals. His salt and pepper hair had almost strategic gray highlights and refined haircut with each hair in place. He was wearing a classy gray raincoat with a tan and navy blue striped scarf. His suit was navy blue with pinstripes and coordinated perfectly with his white and tan striped shirt and wine and navy blue tie. The image was one of opulence.

He nodded his head in acknowledgment, and shook his head in opposition. His voice seemed cultured as he said, "Yes, I'll do that. Well, just be patient and let's give the medicine time to work before we make any decisions. How are the kids? I'm sure it they're shaken up by the whole ordeal. To see a family member go through this is a traumatic experience."

You could see the people in line drop their heads in sympathy; an ill loved one is a delicate situation. Everyone seemed to be patient, except for the thin woman next in line. The man continued his conversation.

"We all love her, but we can't just throw money at this. Quality of life is important, too. Why should we pay good money for her to live miserably? Oh, now I sound like the bad guy, but someone has to be a voice of reason in this situation. It's truly dreadful, but is it for her or for us?" He paused briefly and suddenly the caring, concerned, and kind gentleman changed from Dr. Jekyll to Mr. Hyde. His calm demeanor receded, and with pure fury he responded, "I never cared for the four-legged, barking, incontinent, walking germ with fur. If it were up to me, we would remedy the problem with a gallon of antifreeze. Surely it costs less than those expensive hacks that couldn't become real doctors! An MRI for a dog! I hope she takes her last breaths tonight, and you and those spoiled brats can go right along with her! I'll call from my cellphone when I leave this Podunk land of outhouses and can get a signal."

As he slammed the phone down, he turned to face a crowd of onlookers amazed at the rant he just released. With his head held high and a posture of vindication, he stared back at the crowd. His nose turned up, he walked around the side of the building to a more than modest luxury car. He swung the driver's side back door open and took off his raincoat. His eyes never left the crowd. He reached inside and removed a coat hanger. After hanging his coat, he slammed the back door and opened the front door. He jumped into the driver's seat, cranked the car, and sped away, heading in the direction from which the traveller came.

The thin lady in line grabbed the phone immediately. She picked up the receiver and deposited coins, banging on the buttons of the phone as she dialed. The phone rung as she impatiently waited on an answer. She wasn't dressed for the weather, wearing only a dirty A-shirt and a pink, thin, short-sleeved shirt with lace around the bottom. It looked as if she had not eaten in days. With her short blond hair, the right clothes, and a soap-infused hose down, she would be model material, but at the moment it was evident that she had suffered the same plight as the traveler. She pressed the lever to reset the call. Her fingers hit the coin return before the coins dropped, and she quickly retrieved them and placed the call again. Again, it appeared no one had answered.

As she attempted to place a third call, the big, burly man next in line yelled in a hearty southern accent, "Com' on Missy, there is others that need that phone you seemed to be so fond of."

She ignored him and continued inserting coins and dialing the number. Suddenly, she spoke into the phone. "Hey!" Yeah, it's me... I need you." She paused, and then said, "I know my credit is no good but—" She paused to listen, then responded, "You all I got. Nobody else takes care of me like you do." She turned to look to see who was looking at her. She turned her back to the big fellow and continued to speak softly. The only understandable words were, "You're so good to me, I'll be there." She hung up the phone, looked at the big man, and said, "Here's the phone you're so fond of." She walked off. The traveler watched her as she disappeared into the rain soaked night.

The big man was dressed in traditional trucker garb—dark blue jeans, a blue and white plaid flannel shirt, and a dirty baseball cap with a net back and the name of a trucking company written in orange letters. His belt buckle could have been a champion wrestler's belt. He walked up, deposited his money, and dialed. The phone was immediately picked up.

As southern as he could offer he said, "Hey there!

It's so good to hear your voice. I can't get you off my mind, and I can't wait till I get back. Thought I'd bounce back into your court."

He leaned against the wall with his back to the traveler, as if to settle in for a long conversation. The man continued to talk, giggling and schmoozing with the person on the other end. The traveler thought of a conversation he had with a friend. The two of them became friends under unlikely conditions. They worked at a convenience store together, but only saw one another in passing. Once there was a blizzard that packed 2 feet of snow onto his city. The small convenience store was owned by a tightwad who insisted on him remaining past his shift to patrol for shoplifters, as he was afraid there would be looting with so much snow. The other person on duty made it to work 3 hours late.

When he walked in he was also drunk, and not capable of staying on his feet for 10 minutes, let alone 12 hours. He was tall and red-headed with freckles and a beer belly. He was a man who knew more little known facts than glaringly obvious information. He was your traditional slacker, and it was evident when looking at his wardrobe; during the blizzard he had on a pair of worn flip flops, a pair of shredded, stone-washed jeans, and a dark green T-shirt that read, "Genius

Inside."

The traveler was furious that he had to do his work after working a 10-hour shift. The other employee sat behind the bullet-proof glass watching for shoplifters when he wasn't dozing or seeing double. The traveler asked him to go and stock the beverages, as he thought the cold of the cooler would help him ease his drunken state. The employee went into the back of the cooler and worked tepidly, stocking the soft drinks, juices, and dairy. Suddenly, there was a large crash in the cooler. The traveler remained at the cash register attending to customers.

Once the store was empty, he locked the door and went to the cooler. The employee laid on the floor with a broken neck of a beer bottle next to his hand.

The traveller said angrily, "Get up! I can't believe you're still trying to drink!" The man didn't respond. He yelled again, "Get up! This is your shift. I've been here for over 14 hours, and I'm not pulling my load and yours! You come in here wasted and worthless for what? For what?"

The man said almost inaudibly, "She left me. I did all I could. I tried as hard as I could, and it wasn't enough." He began sobbing.

The traveler, now realizing the employee's underlying problem, told him to get up, as it wasn't safe to be lying in the cooler drunk. He reached out to help him, and the employee yelped in pain. He rolled over, and the traveller spotted the bottom of the broken beer bottle; it was sunken into his side, directly by his kidney.

"Ohhh! I've done it now!" He clenched his side in agony.

The traveler screamed, "No!"

It was too late. The employee grabbed the bottle and tore it away from his side.

Blood started to flow immediately after he removed the bottle glass. The traveler ran to the front and grabbed the phone. He called 911, but due to the blizzard, he was placed on hold. He ran back to the cooler to find the employee bleeding profusely. He ran to the supply closet and grabbed several clean towels.

As he arrived in the cooler, the operator said, "911 what's the emergency?"

He rattled off the address and responded, "I have a man in our cooler who has fallen on a broken beer bottle. He has a deep laceration to his side. The bottom of the bottle was about 4 inches in and when he pulled it out he started bleeding. It's a lot of blood."

The rest was a blur, but the operator walked him through applying pressure to the wound and keeping the man conscious. It seemed to take forever before the EMS and fire department arrived, when in reality it was only 30 minutes. They quickly came in, removed the employee from the cooler, and whisked him away to the hospital.

A few days passed before the traveler returned to work, and it was then he heard that the employee was in the hospital and had been fired for coming to work drunk. Sadly, the employee's kidney was torn to shreds during the accident and had been removed. His other kidney was weak and wasn't strong enough to compensate for the extra load.

He went to the hospital to visit the employee. He walked into the room and was greeted by the rhythmic beeping and hissing of medical devices. He walked to the bed and stared at the man as he lay there. While visiting, a woman walked into the room.

She was a large woman with big features. She had

big eyes, big lips, and she was tall and solid. Her obviously dyed her hair was jet black and pulled back. Her rocker jacket and jeans gave her a rebellious appearance. She looked at the traveler and said, "Excuse me who are you?"

He responded, "Hello. I worked with him. I was there the night it happened. I just wanted to check on him to see how he was doing." She walked toward him and gave him a hug, then began to cry inconsolably.

"I told him that he was too good to work at that convenient store. I told him so many times that wasn't using his college degree because he didn't want the responsibility. He's a drunk, but I love him. I didn't know he was in the hospital until today. I went by our apartment and his mother was there. The day this happened, I was so angry. I told him I had enough and I was leaving. I packed a bag and went to my mom's house. He was drinking when I left, and I know he was two sheets to the wind when he got to work. And now to think he might die because of me."

The traveler consoled her and told her it wasn't her fault. If she ever expected him to take responsibility, she first had to make him responsible.

The man woke up looking at the woman. He smiled and said, "Hey you. I love you. I'm sorry that this happened. I planned to grow old with you, but I may not be able to do that now. You are the love of my life, and I want you to know that and even if I die today, I love you."

The woman leaned over the bed, hugged him, and cried. As the man in the bed was hugging the woman, he noticed the traveler sitting next to him. He said, "Whoa! There's Rubber man! Hey man, I owe you my life. I wouldn't be here if you wasn't so awesome." He reached out to shake his hand while the woman was still laying on him.

The lady stood and faced the traveler and said, "You're the one that saved his life? Why didn't you tell me? We owe you so much. You gotta come over for dinner, and I won't take no for an answer. As soon as he's outta here, we're treating you to a feast."

The traveler said, "No, I did what anyone would have done. I'm just glad you're better." Looking at the patient, he said, "I'll let you get some time with one another. Tell me if there's anything that I can do. I'll write my number on the board." He wrote his phone number on the board and left to go to work.

The next day, the phone rang. It was the lady from the hospital. She was hysterical and asked the traveler if he was willing to be tested to be a kidney donor. If her husband didn't get a kidney soon, it would be too late. Reluctantly, he went to the clinic to get tested. He thought it was a 1 in a million shot that he would be a match.

The test came back. He was a match.
At that time, he wasn't in the market for any surgery. His employer was angry that the convenience store would be short staffed for a few weeks and warned him that he might not have a job after he recovered, but he went ahead and did what he thought he would want someone to do for him.

While recovery for his new found friend was almost immediate, the traveler had complications. It took almost two months to begin feeling like himself. The two men bonded, and became like brothers. His new friend affectionately called him, "Rubber Man."

One day, the traveller asked, "Why do you call me 'Rubber Man'?"

The man replied, "If it weren't for you, I would have never bounced back."

After 10 years of friendship, the two had a big argument about the friend's drinking problem. The friend continued to drink after the surgery, and more often than not went overboard. When he was drunk he was loud, boisterous, and would normally tell too much information. Usually the information was other people's information. The two didn't speak to one another for weeks. One night, as he was heading back from a bar, the friend walked out in front of a taxi cab. He suffered massive head trauma and died instantly.

Standing at the phone booth, back in reality, the traveler thought of the brutal words he said and regretted not being able to ask for forgiveness. He realized he was never given the opportunity to forgive. That was when he realized that he didn't know who to call. He would have called his friend, but he was gone.

The big man dug in, as if he would be on the phone for a long time. The traveler reminded him of his presence with a long sigh. The big man looked at him and shook his head back and forth, disapproving of his appearance. The two stood there staring at each other as the big man continued his conversation only responding, "Yep," every so often. The big man could see the impatience growing in the face of the traveler. He begin concluding his call saying, "Well there's a fella standing here giving me the stink eye. I'm sure he has a rather important call to make." He paused, and then said, "No, no, he ain't no problem. I just wanna know, when can I come see you? Well I ain't gonna have that surgery. I'm gonna wait and see what happens. I ain't never been one for going under the knife, and I ain't about to start now." He paused again and said, "Yeah it's spreadin', but it's a lot of me to go around. I got faith. Lemme let cha go and let this brother use the phone. I love you. Bye."

The big man hung up the phone and said to the traveler, "Sorry it took so long. I had a lot of catching up to do." He smiled and said, "You be safe and keep faith," as he walked back towards the trucks at the diesel island.

The traveler grabbed the phone, reached deep into his pants pockets for change, and came up empty.

"Where's my change? I had a boatload of change."

During the running, crawling, jumping, tumbling and rolling he had lost every coin he had in his pockets. He slammed the phone down simultaneously as the lights at the gas station shut off. "No!"

He ran to the door only to find the young cashier standing in the middle of the store holding the mop. The cashier said "We're closed," as the traveler read his lips. He then reached in his back pocket and pulled out his muddy, wet wallet and retrieved a $20.00 bill holding it to the door.

"I need change for the payphone." He said it loud enough for the cashier to hear and made sure he could read his lips.

The cashier walked close to the door, and once again, said, "We're closed!"

The traveler pleaded, "Please, my car broke down. I need to make a call to get help. I don't even know where I am. Please help me, PLEASE!"

The young man had a medium build and was over tanned. He had ear buds in his ears, and his extra-large shirt was hanging out of his pants and below his employer provided vest. His pants were hanging off of him as if he unbuttoned them after a holiday feast. He walked to the door again and stood there. He looked at the traveler and repeated, "We're closed! We open at 6 tomorrow morning."

The traveler fell to his knees. He shook his head,

not believing the events that had transpired. He couldn't make the phone call that he so desperately wanted to make. He couldn't walk another step. All he wanted was a phone call, and for the person on the other end to tell him it would be okay.

He looked up to find the cashier dancing as he mopped the floors. It was somewhat comical to watch, as the guy appeared to be doing a hip hop dance routine that he never practiced, and his moves were as graceful as a boat anchor on land. Oblivious to the fact he was being watched, he spun and kicked the mop bucket splashing water all over the soft drink dispenser and cabinets. He grabbed two hot dogs from the steamer in one hand and held them above the mop as if they were a microphone and sand. He kicked the mop to the floor with the tip of the handle facing the door and began to sing into the hot dogs as if it were his solo. Then he bit the hot dogs in half.

When he reached down to get the mop, he saw the traveler still at the door. He was visibly embarrassed, but he took one ear bud out and said, "Hey idiot! I said we're closed!" Without losing a step he turned, picked up the mop, and continued his duties. The traveler sat on the curb outside the store with his face in his hands. He was completely out of gas.

As he sat, he heard a car pull up accompanied by a rather loud dispatcher of a radio. He looked up; it was the police. The officer was a large black man. He slammed the car in park and bolted from the car. He was huge, at least 6'8", and appeared as wide as he was tall.

With his hand on his gun, he approached the traveler and said, "Good evening, sir. The store is closed. I'm gonna have to ask you to move on."

The traveler said in a run on sentence, "Sir I need help, please help me, my car broke down, I walked up here, I lost my change, I have a twenty dollar bill but I can't make a phone call, I got crap all over me, I think I was being chased by wolves and—"

The officer grabbed the radio and murmured something into it. "Sir, have you been drinking or taking any drugs tonight?"

The traveler answered as if he were insulted, "No! I'm beat! I just told you, I got crap on me, walked from my car, lost my coins and tumbled down the hill in the cow pasture, I got cut on the fence in the pasture. I need help!" He didn't realize that nothing he was saying was making sense.

The officer told him, "Just calm down and let me see your license." The traveler pulled out his wallet, retrieved his license, and began wiping the foreign debris from it before handing it to the officer. Shortly, two other police cars pulled up. The officer waited for the other officers to join him, and they surrounded the traveler.

The officer said, "You're a long way from home. Where are you heading?"

Once again the man began explaining. "My car broke down. I'm driving coast to coast. This has been the worst day of my life. Not one thing has went right." One of the officers asked him for a description of his car and where it had broken down. The man gave the description of the car, but he couldn't give an accurate description of where the car broke down.

The officer radioed and gave the description of the car. Shortly the dispatcher said, "A car fitting that description was towed to the yard earlier today. We've been checking to see if it's stolen, but it came back clean."

The traveler jumped to his feet and said, "It's been towed? Great! Now I have no car, no nothing."

He really wasn't aware of how threatening he was to the officers. The officer again told him to calm down and asked, "How can we help you?"

The man said, "I just want to get this crap off of me. I need a doctor for the cuts on my back. I'm tired hungry and thirsty, and I want to make a phone call but I only have a twenty. I need change."

The officer dug in his pocket and removed 75 cents. He told the man, "We can do this two ways. I can either take you to the precinct and you can stay with us until we know what's going on with you, or I can give you enough for a phone call and then you go on your way. Which one will it be?"

The man calmly said, "I'd like to make a phone call, and I then I will leave. Can you please tell me where I may find a hotel?"

"If you want to go to the hotel, I'll take you up there. You can make your phone call from your room."

The traveler responded ecstatically, "Please! I just want to clean up and get some rest." The officer escorted him to his car and placed him in the back.

The hotel was only a ¼ mile up the highway, but before they turned out of the parking lot the officer noticed the smell coming from the traveler. He rolled down all the windows as he drove up the highway. When they arrived at the motel—a small, family run operation—the officer got out and released the traveler from the back of the cruiser. He asked him, "Am I going to have any more problems out of you tonight?"

The traveler responded, "No Sir, I just want a shower, some food, and a bed."

The officer returned to the driver seat and looked at the traveler and said, "Be safe and keep faith." He closed the door and slowly drove off, waiting for the traveler to go inside the motel lobby.

GREEN PASTURES MOTEL

The man walked into the motel, looking as rag tag as they come. He was met by the smell of garlic and bleach. The low pile red carpet—briefly chic and at the top of fashion in 1977— had seen better days. There was nothing special here, just a small sitting area and a tourism brochure holder. He thought to himself, *What tourist attractions are around here?*

A charming Indian man wearing a pair of wire rim glasses was behind the counter. His comb over hairstyle attempted to hide his balding locks. He wore a yellow polo shirt and was very cordial as he greeted the traveler.

"Good evening, sir. Welcome to Green Pastures. How may I assist you?"

The traveler, who was checking his wallet, simply replied, "A room if you got one."

The innkeeper said, "I have one room left." They agreed on the price, and the traveler handed the innkeeper his credit card. The innkeeper said, "I'm sorry sir, but we don't take this card. If you have one of the ones we take or cash, the room is yours. Or you may use the ATM."

He was not surprised by the inability to use his card, as it had been rejected in other establishments. Based on his day, it was something he expected. He went to the ATM; it was out of order.

The traveller went back to the counter and said, "Your ATM says it's out of service. Is there another ATM close by?"

The innkeeper said, "Yes the bank is right down the road."

"How far down the road?"

"Oh, about 5 miles down." He said, "but I'm not driving you."

The traveler was blown away by how his night was transpiring. As he looked around, he saw a sign for Western Union on the door. He had an idea: he would Western Union himself the money needed from his credit card.

He asked the innkeeper, "Do you have a business center with a computer with internet access?"

The innkeeper answered, "Certainly, but it's only for tenants."

He explained his grand scheme to Western Union himself the money. The innkeeper allowed him to use the computer, and soon the money was on its way. He waited 15 minutes as the website stated, then asked the man to check for the transfer.

He said, "Certainly. ID is required to make the transaction."

The traveler suddenly realized that he never got his license back from the police officer. He sighed and asked the hotel innkeeper to call the police department. The innkeeper was becoming impatient with him. "Sir I can no longer help you. I must ask you to leave."

The traveller explained, "No, the police dropped me off here, and they kept my license."

This really didn't build the confidence of the innkeeper. Looking at the traveler's appearance and frustrated with him being unable to pay, he picked up the phone and called the police.

"911, what is your emergency?"

"Yes, I have a man in the lobby at Green Pastures who refuses to leave. He has asked me to call the police, and I'm not sure of what he wants." The dispatcher stayed on the line with the innkeeper and told him someone was on the way.

She asked him if the man appeared to be dangerous, he told her he wasn't sure, but he was very dirty and kept pacing back and forth, shaking his head as if he was talking to an imaginary person.

The traveler realized this wasn't working in his favor, and he walked out the front door to wait for the officer to pull up.

Within minutes, the same officer from the store pulled up. He jumped out of the car and said, "Put your hands in the air, turn around, and get on your knees. I told you I didn't want no more trouble out of you tonight." He grabbed his arm and slapped the handcuffs on.

The traveler protested, "I didn't do nothing. You have my license. I couldn't get the money for the room because I didn't have my license." The officer grabbed his shirt pocket; the license was there. He unbuttoned the shirt pocket and removed the license. He continued to place the handcuffs on the traveler, helped him to his feet, and placed him in the car.

He went inside the motel. After a brief conversation with the innkeeper, he returned to the car. He sat in the driver seat and said, "OK I have your license. He has your Western Union. He will rent you the room. Will I have any more trouble from you tonight?"

The traveler mumbled as if he had lost all the fight that was in him, "No, sir."

The officer hopped from the driver's seat and opened the back door. He removed the hand cuffs. The traveler started walking toward the front door of the motel when the officer said, "Hey, you're forgetting something." He walked towards him and handed him his license. "Your identification. That is what this is about isn't it?"

The traveler smiled and said, "Yes, I would like to have my identity back, and it starts with a shower."

The officer smiled and told him, "Be safe and keep faith. You'll be better soon sir after a shower and some rest."

The traveler walked into the motel and to the counter. He passed his identification to the innkeeper, and he worked intensely at the computer. He passed a sheet of paper under the window to the traveler, who signed the document and passed it back. The innkeeper slipped the cash and room register slip under the window. The traveler signed it and passed it back, along with the payment. The innkeeper gave him the key and said, "I'm sorry for the time it has taken. Your room is on the top floor; it's the last door on the back. The elevator is broken, so unfortunately you must use the steps. Would you like a wakeup call?"

The traveler said, "Yes, 7 AM, please."
He walked outside and started up the steps. He went to the third floor and walked to the last door. He unlocked the door.

The room was dark and cold. He felt the wall next to the door until he found the light switch. The carpet, décor, and bedding were ripped directly from the early 80s. Nauseating crimson and hunter green carpets extended to the back wall, which was covered with a large mirror, laminate countertop, and sink. There was an ice bucket and coffee maker sitting on the counter, along with a tiny bar of soap, miniature shampoo, conditioner, and lotion.

He turned and closed the crimson curtains. The heating unit came to life when he switched the setting to high. It roared and growled as it blew even colder air than the room already contained. He caught a glimpse of himself in the mirror and began to laugh at the amount of muck he had all over himself. He placed his hands on the sink and dropped his head. The smell of dirt and debris from the unused Air Conditioner filled the room, but he took that as a good sign that the heater did indeed work. The scent of the unclean heater soon became unbearable. He opened the door to the room and allowed the odor to escape as he got some air.

The door next to him opened, and an older lady emerged. She was 4 foot nothing, with her hair in a bonnet and face still made up from earlier in the day. She wore a terry cloth robe that was pulled around her so tightly it appeared to choke her neck.

She looked at the stranger and said, "No smoking! These are non-smoking rooms. I told him that I couldn't be around any cigarette smoke. If you don't put it out I'm calling the front desk and telling him you're smoking in that room."

He smirked and said, "It's not me smoking. It's that dirty heater in my room. This room must have been vacant for a long time. The odor was almost choking me. That's why I'm standing out here." She looked at him and didn't respond. She slammed the door a small dog begin to bark.

After a few minutes, the smell of the heater subsided, and he stepped back in the room. He sat in the chair at the table and began taking off his jacket, shoes, and other clothes. He leaned back and took a deep breath with his eyes closed and head back. The phone rang, and he picked it up. "Hello?"

The innkeeper was on the phone. He said, "Yes, this is management. The person next door has reported that you are smoking. Please extinguish your cigarette. I ask that you do not smoke in the room. There is a smoking area around back by the pool."

He wanted to tell him and the old lady how he really felt, but instead said, "Thank you," and hung up the phone.

He went to the bathroom and turned on the shower. He admired how the mold accented grout and dated decorum. He then realized that he had nothing to wear.

He thought about being hungry and thirsty. He remembered a pizza coupon sitting on the nightstand. He called the pizza place and ordered a double pepperoni and a 2 liter of Coca-Cola Classic. He listened as the order taker tallied the order and responded with the price and an estimated delivery time of 1 hour. Once again, he just smiled. He knew that soon, all of his troubles would be over and he'd have a new set in the morning.

Still hungry and thirsty he put the nasty pants, shirt, and jacket back on. He went down the stairs and into the mezzanine. There was a laundry room, ice machine, drink machine, and snack machine. He pulled the 4 dollars that he received as change from the motel innkeeper. He slid the dollar in the bill receptor of the snack machine, and it slid it out. He slid it in again; it slid back out. He turned the bill around and tried again. The machine paused. It considered his dollar for a few seconds, but inevitably slid it out. He tried another bill with the same results.

He decided to try the drink machine. He placed the dollar in the bill receptor, and it accepted it. However, each drink was $1.25. He added another dollar and pressed the button for Coca-Cola Classic, but the light indicated it was out. He went for Pepsi, and the machine delivered a Diet 7 Up and 75 cents change.

Everything he wanted in the vending machine was a dollar or more, so he decided his only recourse was to buy another soft drink. He slid his money in and decided to take a gamble and pressed as many buttons as he could. A Coca-Cola Classic emerged from the machine.

He laughed "Ha Ha! My LUCK is turning around." The drink machine dropped another 75 cents, and he moved to the snack machine. He deposited his money and pressed the E15 selection for a Snickers. He couldn't wait to have what he believed was the most awesome candy bar ever invented.

The candy bar dropped and grabbed it, pulled the wrapper off, and immediately began biting the bar as if he hadn't eaten in weeks. He turned to go up the steps.

The innkeeper was outside. He looked at him and said, "The smoking area is this way."

The traveler smiled, "Thank you," he said through a mouth full of chocolate, caramel, nougat, and peanuts.

He carried the Diet 7 Up and Coca-Cola Classic back up to his room. He unlocked the door and went inside. The room was now feeling a lot cozier. He sat down, opened the Coke, and slurped it down, then tried to think of a way that he could take his clothes to the laundry. He had no other clothes.

Once again, he grabbed the key and went downstairs to the front desk. He pulled a twenty from his pocket and asked for change with coins so he may use the laundry. He received change and went back upstairs to the cozy room.

At this point, the room felt like a 5-star hotel room when compared to the rest of his day. He pulled off his jacket and sat back, placing his head in his hands. He drifted off quietly into the peace of the hum of the heating unit and the comfort of the room.

Boom! Boom! Boom! Boom! The door rattled. He opened his eyes, not sure how long he had been asleep. He opened the door to find the same teenager from the gas station with a different vest and hat. "You ordered pizza?" he said. He gave him the total and pushed the pizza and 2 liter into his hands. He couldn't possibly hear anything but the loud hip hop music blaring from his ear buds.

The traveler handed him a twenty and said "Keep the change." The young man walked off without a thank you or any acknowledgment.

He sat the pizza box on the table and opened the top. He went to the ice bucket and grabbed a cup shrouded in plastic. The pizza guy must have dropped the cola; as he opened it, the fizz swelled and sprayed him, the foot of the bed, and the pizza. Like it never happen, he poured himself another round of the fizzy drink. He grabbed a slice of pizza, and although it was dripping wet from cola, he devoured half of the slice on his first bite. "Not bad," he said as the merger of the pizza and cola excited his taste buds. With two more bites, the slice was gone. He repeated the process, knocking out 3 slices of pizza.

And now for the moment he had been waiting for. A rush of excitement—or a rush of sugar, carbs, and caffeine—produced a happy feeling, and he couldn't wait to get that shower.
He went to the bathroom and turned the shower handle. The water poured out was as cold as the Bering Sea. He waited for the water to get hot as he removed his shirt, pants, underwear, socks and shoes. He grabbed a towel and thought this was probably the best time to take the clothes to the laundry. They could wash while he was in the shower, and he would place them in the dryer when he got out of the shower.

He grabbed a towel and wrapped it around his lower extremities. He scooped up the clothes and grabbed his key and change, all while holding the towel around him. He somehow awkwardly opened the door and peeked out to see if there were any people outside. He saw no one.

As quickly as he could, with the wind encroaching on the warmth of his body he snuck quietly down to the mezzanine and in the laundry room. He opened the washer and forced the clothing through the opening. He turned to the laundry vending unit and placed 4 quarters in to get laundry detergent. The detergent dropped and he retrieved it, tearing the box open and emptying the contents into the washer. He then decided to buy another box of detergent since his clothes were so soiled. He emptied the box and closed the top. He remembered that his key was in the hand with the clothes. He opened the washer and dug through its contents until he found the key. He placed 4 more quarters in the washer set the unit to HOT and pressed the start button. Nothing happened, until he closed the lid. Water began filling the tub of the washer. He again peeked out, then ran up the steps and back in his room. Once inside, he shook in protest of the cold.

In the bathroom, he was greeted by steam coming from the shower. He removed the towel, stepped behind the shower curtain and placed his full body directly under the head of the shower. He stood there as the warm water ran through his hair and down his chest. When it hit his back, he winced as it trickled into the cuts and scratches;

exciting the nerve endings to alert him to where the integrity of his skin had been compromised.

It was if he could feel the day leaving him. He looked down to find the crap and mud colored water making its way down the drain. He just stood there. The water ran over his cuts and gave him a good-hurt feeling. The idea of cleansing was more than enough to be grateful for in the present moment.

As he stood there, he thought of his friend again. He wished there was a way for him to apologize. Who was he to judge him for his drinking? He felt responsible for his untimely demise.

He looked at the scar on his side from the kidney surgery. He remembered drinking beer with his friend at a pool party. Both of them enjoyed swimming and partying. They swore it wasn't a party until the two of them arrived. Their friendship was very close, and it was rare to see one of them without the other.

His friend's wife was usually there also. He really loved and respected their relationship. They were both into metal music. They met as members of a metal band. She played bass guitar, and he played just about any instrument you placed in front of him. Music was a true connection for them.

The traveler wished his relationship was that close, but his then fiancé and he didn't have as much in common as his friend and his wife. The traveler loved his fiancé, but he was a free spirit that enjoyed meeting new people, going out, sports, and the outdoors. She was more of a home body. She enjoyed reading, watching TV, and the arts. A perfect night out for her was seeing an art exhibit, ballet, or schmoozing with socialites in their city. He didn't enjoy it and constantly called her a yuppie brat because of her taste, but he accompanied her to the events because it appeared to make her happy. He loved to see her happy.

At the party, the friend's kidney operation scars were exposed. He had tattoos all around them, but the scars were still apparent. Someone asked him about them.

"I did this in a drunken stupor," he replied, pointing to the beer bottle scars, "but this is where me and Rubber Man used to be Siamese twins. We were joined at the hip in opposite directions. That's why everything he does is backwards."

The memory struck him, and he became overwhelmed with emotions and he began to cry. His tears could not be distinguished from the shower droplets. He cried, "I miss you man. I'm sorry. I'm sorry I was such a butt."

He began to think of not just his day, but his current presence. He was unemployed, and his relationship with his fiancé was in shambles. He had lost touch with his family and was unable to find his place in the world. His car which—the first one he owned that wasn't a rolling disaster—was going to be repossessed at any time. He and his fiancé were about to be evicted from their home. There wasn't one bill that wasn't behind. Debt collectors called him constantly. The credit card he used to get the room had $212 more dollars before it was over limit. He had to change to a cheaper cell phone and didn't even have cable. He was underwater.

He was paralyzed with nothing but his tear ducts pumping uncontrollably. He shook his head and watched as the dirty brown water slowly started flowing clear. He was unable to stop the rush of emotions. This shower was washing away more than the physical dirt; there was moral, emotional, and spiritual being moved by the droplets.

He felt the water temperature begin to cool. He stepped out of the shower and grabbed the shampoo and conditioner from the countertop. He began washing his hair. The feel of the shampoo and water made his skin slick, and he started feeling more refreshed. He scrubbed his body, finding clusters of mud and dirt and watching as it disappeared down the drain. He was unable to scrub his back, as some of the wounds were deep and hurt as the towel passed over them. He resigned to rubbing soap on the towel and squeezing to allow the soap and water combination to run down his back. He rinsed off. The water was still hot, but not steaming. He massaged the conditioner into his hair and began scrubbing his body for a second time, still finding small clusters of mud and dirt. The water coming from the shower was soon cool. He continued to rinse, enjoying the feeling of the cool water as it removed the soap, dirt, and pains.

He stepped out of the shower, and grabbed a fresh towel. While drying, he still found deposits of dirt but very little. He felt a lot better than when he got in the shower. He stepped out of the bathroom and sat at the foot of the bed. The mattress felt lumpy, but he couldn't wait until he could lay in it and rest. He took the towel and dried his lower legs and feet. He then thought about his clothes in the washer.

He grabbed his change and his keys and scampered to the laundry room. He quickly retrieved the clothes and threw them in the dryer. He looked at each article of clothing; it was almost impossible to tell they were previously dirty, but the cuts and tears from the fence episode were still evident. He looked at the vending station at first about to purchase dryer sheets and decided against them. He placed 75 cents in the dryer, set it to hot, and pressed start. He crept up the steps unsuspected and went into his room. He removed the towel and lay back on the bed. It didn't take him long to recognized that he was drifting to sleep. He picked up the phone and called the front desk. When the innkeeper picked up, he asked how long the dryer usually took to dry.

The innkeeper responded, "One hour sir." The traveler asked him to wake him in an hour so he may retrieve his clothes. As soon as he hung up the phone, he was asleep.

The ringing phone shocked the traveler from his slumber and he answered.

"This is your wake up, sir," the innkeeper said. The traveler thanked him and asked him to reset the wake up for 9am. He sprung to his feet and bolted out the door, realizing too late that he didn't have his key. He went downstairs to the laundry room and realized he also needed his key to enter the laundry room.

He sighed, knowing that entering the lobby would cause a problem. He walked to the front only to find people standing in the lobby. He smiled politely, holding his towel closely, and walked into the lobby. A lady in her 50s or early 60s stood outside with a look of shock on her face. He walked to the counter and said, "My clothes are in the laundry, and I locked my key in my room."

The innkeeper looked at him and said, "Sir, you can't walk around wearing a towel. Please go back to your room."

"I locked my key in my room. My clothes are in the laundry room. May I please have a key to my room? The innkeeper looked at the face of the lady outside, then back to the traveler. He picked up the phone and once again dialed 911.

The traveler begged, "Sir please don't call the police. It was an honest mistake. You saw how filthy my clothes were. I had to wash them. I was going to the laundry room to get my clothes, but the door closed before I grabbed my key. Please!"

The innkeeper hung up the phone and gave him another key. He told him, "I don't want to see you again tonight. If I get one more complaint about you streaking or smoking, I will call the police." He thanked the innkeeper and took the key to the laundry room.

The door to the laundry room closed, and he gathered his clothes from the dryer. He took off his towel and began stepping into his underwear when the door flew open. It was the lady from phone booth at the gas station. He stood there, embarrassed, as he pulled his underwear up.

She stared back at him. She was wearing nothing but a towel that covered her from her chest to almost her knees.

He stuttered as he said, "Forgive me I, I..."

She responded, "Don't you try anything funny, or I'll put this key through your eye!"

He again started, "I don't want no trouble. Let me get my towel and clothes, and I'll be out of your way." She stood there and watched him intensely as he wrapped the towel around himself and gathered the rest of his clothes. "I'm going to put on my shirt, if that's okay with you. It's cold out there."

"None of this is okay with me. I didn't have no desire to see you naked in the laundry room tonight. All I wanna do is wash my clothes," she replied.

He put his shirt on, took the rest of his clothes and said, "I apologize. Have a good night," he said as he walked out of the laundry room.

As the door closed, he turned to find his friend the police officer standing behind him. "Boy, you and trouble is like my wife and shoes, you can't get enough can you?" He shook his head and opened his mouth to explain, and the officer said, "Shh!" You and your lady friend in the room there are about to go to jail. I tried to help both of you. I didn't want to take either of you to jail. "He beat on the laundry room door, "Open the door police."

She opened the door with the towel wrapped around her, recognizing the officer's voice. She exclaimed, "I ain't done nothing. I'm just trying to wash my clothes. You saw how dirty I was."

The officer said, "Stand right here, Mr. Peek-a-boo. Com'on outta there young lady. You and him been raising cane all night. I tried to be nice, but now people calling hangin' up the phone and I find you two lovebirds out here wearing nothing but towels. The pool is closed, and only a fool would be in the pool tonight. What's wrong with y'all? You gotta room!" In sync both of them started saying, "I just wanted to wash my clothes, you know how dirty I was, I came down to get my clothes washed."

The traveler continued on, "And I locked my key in my room. I went up front to get another. The lady outside acted like I was performing a strip tease, I just wanted my clothes so I can go to bed."

The woman said "This moron has had the washer and dryer all to himself for the last hour. I ain't got no other clothes, and they were filthy. I walk down here and he's in the laundry room changing."

The traveler wanted to clear up any misconceptions so he added. "The door was closed, I put on my underwear and I turn around and there she is—"

The officer said, "SHUT UP!" He shot both of them a look that could silence a crying newborn. "I get it both of you have been catching it. We all in the same boat, but y'all are causing problems. I'm gonna let you go one more time, but if I see either of you again, I'm arresting you on the spot."

The traveler said, "Sir thank you, I am not trying to be—"

"Shut up and just go," said the officer.

The woman said, "Yes sir," and she closed the door to the laundry room, as the traveler disappeared as fast as possible up the stairs to the comfort of his room.

He threw his clothes on the foot of the bed. They remarkably remained balled in the same knot. He took off his shirt, turned off the light, and climbed back into bed.

Three sharp taps came at the door, followed by "Housekeeping!"

He was slow to awake and thought he was only dreaming. He laid there in a trance. He was conscious of the housekeeper, but he was unable to move. The knock came again, and he answered in his mind but could tell he was still in between dreaming and consciousness. He could hear as the key in the lock and the door opening. A small Indian woman opened the door. She said, "Housekeeping," as she walked in the room. The traveler was barely able to raise his head, when she said, "Oh, okay. I come back."

He looked at the alarm clock on the nightstand. The time read 8:34AM. He had 26 minutes to sleep, and he was going to make it count. His head crashed back into the pillow, and he covered his head with the comforter in an attempt to go back to sleep before his brain kicked into gear.

It was too late. His brain woke to frantic queries about his car. Where was it? How long would it take to fix? Most importantly, how much would it cost?

A second thread of doubts began. What if the car can't be repaired? What if it has been reported to the loan company and is now repossessed? If it's repossessed, how will he make it to his destination? What if his personal items have been taken from the car?

A third thread was processing. Who can help you? Who can you call?

A fourth thread: Why should anyone help you? When are you going to get a job? How will you pay your bills? How will you get to a job once your car is gone? How do you repair your relationship? What if you have to start over?

He snatched the pillow from under him and covered his head with it as if someone else was in the room asking him the questions. Peeking at the alarm clock, he saw that he had 23 minutes before his scheduled wake up call. He took a deep breath to calm down. He couldn't answer any of those questions, and right now wasn't the time to try. The wounds on his back were extremely sore. He was sore all over from the physical exhaustion he went through on yesterday. Unable to keep his mind from churning questions, he went ahead and got out of bed. He put his shirt on and sat on the bed, scratching his head. He walked to the counter and ran the water until it was hot. He threw water on his face. He stared in the mirror and shook his head. The face was familiar but he didn't know who the person was in the mirror.

The questions continued to burn in his head. He grabbed the bundle of clothes, pulled the pants from the jacket, and put them on. They were quite wrinkled. He only had one sock. He had put two socks in the dryer, but he was unsure of how many were there when he retrieved his clothes. He put on the one sock and his shoes. That morning was far colder than the night before. As the sun came up, it created a fog, and each blade of grass was armored with shiny dew.

He went downstairs to the laundry room to see if his sock was possibly down there. He walked in only, to be reunited with the lady from last night. "You following me? She asked, looking at him with her death squint.

He rolled his eyes and shook his head without responding. "Did I leave a sock down here last night?" he asked.

"I ain't got your sock, don't want your sock and if you don't stop following me, I'm gonna sock you!" She responded. He sighed and turned to walk out the door. She yelled, "Wait, I found your sock."

He turned around and faced her. She smiled and giggled and said, "Turn around."

He looked at her and said, "Please just give me the sock and I'm gone on my way."

She continued to smile and said "I'll show you the sock if you'll turn around." Tired of playing games he walked out of the laundry room, furious at her for playing with him.

She followed him out of the room and walked up behind and they were both shocked as she reached toward his back to remove one sock from the back of his shirt held firmly in place by static cling. She jumped and so did he. He turned around, and she was standing there holding his sock with a red marking.

She looked at him and said, "You need to get that cut on your back checked out, because it's bleeding.

He turned around and asked, "Is it really bad? It does hurt a lot."

She looked at him and said, "Somebody stabbed you in the back? It don't look good, but I can't tell through your shirt." She lifted his shirt to see several scars, neatly and evenly spaced, complimented by scratches with similar spacing. There were three wounds that were long and appeared deep about three inches each. "You been cut up good. But I think you'll be alright. That my professional medical opinion. How you do all this?"

He was sure the medical opinion part was sarcasm. He pulled his shirt down and responded, "It's a long story involving a barbed wire fence." He turned to her and said, "Thank you."

They both walked to the lobby, where a continental breakfast was being served. They walked in to find several people inside the lobby. Small children were running everywhere. Everyone was dressed in western outfits, cowboy hats, and boots. They wore all of the accessories, ornate spurs and buckles, chaps, and sheriff badges. It was almost as if they had stepped back in time, except for the number of teens and adults standing in the middle of the room with their heads down, searching for signals on their cell phones.

The continental breakfast was practically untouched, but the servers were quite busy keeping the supply of coffee, milk, and juice stocked to meet the demand. They both walked to the countertop, which held a display of items. There were breads, danishes, doughnuts, rolls—some drizzled with icing—fritters, and bear claws. There was yogurt, butter, milk, packets of oatmeal, grits, cream of wheat, apples, oranges, and grapes. Like a carousel, servers rotated empty pitchers and carafes of apple, orange, and cranberry juice, regular and decaf coffee, and hot water.

The traveler picked up one of the thin 4" Styrofoam appetizer plates, and surveyed the spread. He reached for a fritter and received a sharp strike to his wrist. He crunched his brow and looked at his new companion as she pointed to the tongs lying next to the tray. She still had that death squint. He picked up the tongs and clasped his selection placing it on his plate. He grabbed a container of yogurt to look healthy. He rarely ate yogurt but why not give it a try today?

He completely skipped the fruit and went straight for a coffee cup. He poured a cup of coffee and immediately gulped down the hot elixir. His eyes bulged, and he quickly swallowed; the coffee burned all the way down. She continued her death squint, slowly shaking her head, as he looked at her.

There were only three tables, each with four of the most uncomfortable looking chairs ever made. He approached a table with three people sitting at the table and asked, "Is this seat taken?" Two of the people shook their heads. The other person's attention was fixed strictly on a cell phone. He sat down and took a large bite from his fritter.

Suddenly the person on the cell phone leaped from their seat, placed the phone to their ear, and rushed out the front door. The woman sat at the table with him, with yogurt, grapes, a small cup of hot water, and a teabag. He didn't look up; he was sure she still had that look on her face. She watched him as he ripped the top off of the yogurt, picked up a spoon, and scooped a small dollop from the top, and placed it in his mouth.

"Where you from?" she asked.

He replied, "Everywhere. You?"

She picked one of the small red grapes from the vine, holding it up and said, "You took the words right outta my mouth."

He looked at her, surprised at the open dialog of small talk, and asked, "Where you headed?"

She nodded her head in the same direction he was traveling and said, "That way."

They both in silence as they ate yogurt. He finally said," My car broke down yesterday, and it's been pretty much downhill from there."

She responded, "I wish it was downhill for me, feel like I been climbing Kilimanjaro. I ain't got no car, I been walking."

He asked, "Do you know how far the mechanic and tow yard could be from here? The police said they towed my car yesterday."

She rolled her eyes and said, "I ain't from around here. Don't know nobody here. I don't even know what you call this place."

Tired of her ability to answer every question with sarcasm, he said, "Watch my seat." He went to the front desk and asked for a phone book. He was handed a small yellow book with the name

"Keep Faith" as the name of the township. He walked back to the table and he realized that everyone he saw previously wasn't telling him to "Keep safe AND keep faith," they were saying "Keep safe IN Keep Faith."

He searched for a towing service. There were only two listed. He asked the person at the table with them for a pen. He jotted down the phone number and address for both listings, and then searched for the mechanic. Again, there were two listed, he took down the information, passed the pen back to the person sitting at the table, and returned the phone book back to the reception area.

He returned to the table, swallowed the last bit of coffee he had, placed the rest of his fritter in his mouth, and pulled his sock out of his jacket pocket. As he put it on, the young lady bumped the table to get his attention. He looked up at her to find the familiar death squint on her face. She stared back at him. She looked at his plate, then him, his sock, then him, then his foot. He took a deep breath and placed his foot back on the floor. He returned his sock to his pocket.

"In this movie, I guess you supposed to be the sarcastic, mother figure that has a bad odor on her top lip?" he said.

She replied as if there were a script. "If I'm playing your mamma in a movie, I would have died from disappointment at the beginning." He couldn't help but snicker, and his smile brought a smile to her face, too.

He made two more trips to the bar for fritters and coffee. He looked at the woman and said, "It's been good. You know, good to have someone to talk to. Thank you. I hope your trip gets easier and you make it to where ever you're going." She sat back in her chair, looked at him, and he could almost see her thoughts on the road ahead bringing fear to her heart as she nodded her head. He smiled and said, "You look much nicer when you're not using your momma death ray laser vision." She smiled as he got up from the table returned to his room.

He walked in the room and sat at the foot of the bed. He picked up the cream colored 80's model phone from the nightstand and dialed 9, then the phone number of the first towing company.

The person picked up immediately. "Yep?" He asked if they towed a car fitting the description of his car. The reply was almost instant. "Nope." He hung up the phone.

He dialed the second tow company. It sounded

like the same person, "Yep?" He described the car and asked if it had been towed. They replied, "Yep."

He asked, "How far are you from Green Pastures Motel?"

The reply was, "Not far at all." He waited for more information, but it never came.

He asked, "What do I need to claim the car?"

The reply was simply, "Cash."

Seeing he wasn't going to get anywhere, he simply responded, "I'm on my way."

The reply was a simple, "Yep."

He removed his shoe from the sock less foot and put his sock on. He took the plastic bag from the ice bucket and placed his remaining pizza in the bag. He folded the bag and placed it inside his inside coat pocket. He picked up the 2 liter and placed it under his arm. He made a final sweep through the room to make sure he had left nothing. With all items in check. He took the keys to the lobby.

He walked in the lobby and stood behind the

woman, who was also checking out. She looked at the innkeeper with a 1000 yard stare as she threw her key on the counter. The innkeeper, very smugly said, "Thank you," as he rolled his eyes.

The innkeeper gave the same look to the traveler as he approached the counter. He asked if he knew how far the towing company was from the motel.

"They are both about 10 miles that way," he said.

"10 miles!" He shook his head looking to the sky as he contemplated a 10 mile walk.

A thin man, with thin black hair holding the hand of a portly redheaded woman at the counter asked him, "Would you like a ride? We're heading that way."

He thanked him, obviously grateful for the offer. The man pointed to a faded white and blue church bus and told him they would be out in just a minute.

The traveler walked out the door and took in the beauty and majesty of the landscape. The colors of the sunlit sky seem to explode as new colors broke through the clouds. He looked around for the young woman, but she was nowhere to be found.

The thin man and portly woman walked out the front door hand in hand. He took long strides, and she shuffled from side to side to keep up. The man allowed the woman to enter the bus first, smiling and saying "After you madam." She smiled. They looked at each other like new found loves. The lady sat in the first seat. He motioned to the traveler, "Com'on aboard take a seat where you like." He smiled and jumped on the bus, sitting near the rear. He didn't think much of religion, and his current situation was certainly not the time to talk about it. The driver started the bus.

The engine sounded like 10 hammers in a clothes dryer. The man placed his head against the seat in front of him looking down at his shoes, not wanting to make eye contact with the lady or the man up front. He didn't want them to ask him to sit up front. He sat there for probably two minutes when he felt someone sit in the seat in front of him. He looked up and recognized the blond haircut.

His head went back down and he said, "You following me?" She smiled but never responded or looked back.

The driver closed the door as the engine revved, and they started down the road. The bus moved at probably 15 miles per hour as they climbed the hill. The traveler stared at his shoes. They were his best and only pair of dress shoes, and they were warped, scratched, and dull from his trek. As the bus started down the hill, it gained momentum.

He could feel as the woman turned around in her seat. She looked at him, but he never raised his head. She sat next to him and said. "Most girls want to be princesses, beauty pageant girls, video vixens, and stuff of the sort. I wanted to be a rodeo clown."

He turned his head and said, "You got on the wrong bus, but you got the hard part of being a clown out of the way." She didn't look amused by his answer; it seemed to sting her pride. Noticing the hurt she felt, he said, "I'm sorry. That was mean. It's been a long, hard trip."

She said, "When I saw you last night, I was about to ask you for pointers on breaking into the industry. You smelled and look like the rear end of a bull."

They both smiled. Up front, the husband and wife duo began singing, "Amazing Grace."

The woman placed her head down also, looked at the traveler, and said, "I don't know the words, but I think they want us to sing along. How far you gotta go?"

He responded, "Not sure. First I gotta check on my car. If I can get it fixed, I'll give you a ride as far as I'm going."

She said, "No. Thank you, but keep your gratitude. I don't think we going the same way. Plus, I got my problems and you got yours. It's best we keep them separate. I don't think you know where you're headed, anyway."

He looked at her, confused. They were both on the same bus, heading in the same direction. How could she say that? He continued to look at his shoes and said, "Your walk, not mine."

They road together in silence for the next 5 miles or more. He listened to the bouncing and squeaking of the bus. His threads of thought about the car, current situation, bills, and unemployment crowded his mind. He thought of his mother. He hadn't spoken to her in a long time. There was no reason other than he refused to pick up the phone and call her.

The bus slowed and turned onto a dirt road. Both of them looked up as the bus came to a complete stop. "Will this help you two?" The driver yelled from the front. Both of them stood to their feet and begin walking towards the front. The woman walked up and first shook the hand of the woman, then the man as she thanked them for the ride. She quickly evacuated the bus. The traveler did the same and asked the location of the towing company. The driver pointed across the road. He nodded in appreciation and stepped down off of the bus. Before pulling off the couple began singing again. The bus continued up the path of the driveway.

He looked as the woman was beginning to walk off. He yelled, "Hey, a fire truck."

She looked and turned to walk back towards him and said, "What?"

He repeated, "A fire truck. I always wanted to be a fire truck when I was little. People respect fire trucks. They're red and shiny. They got all those gauges and hoses. They always keep them clean. You never see a broke down fire truck."

She smiled, turned, and walked down the highway, not saying a word.

THE MECHANICS

The man looked across the highway to see the end of green grass partitioned by a tall chain link fence with barbed wire along the top and pieces of sheet metal blocking the view into the yard. He was looking at a junkyard. As far as he could see there were cars tacked on top of other cars. There was a wooden building in the middle of the yard. The building appeared to be a duplex with one side painted white and the other side painted black.

He ran across the highway and entered the door white door on the left. Inside, there was just enough room to stand at a counter with a window. A big man with rosy cheeks, gray hair, and a beard sat behind the counter, smoking a pipe. He had on dirty blue coveralls filled with oil, dirt, and grease, a sure sign he worked on cars. He sat there holding some small device that could be either a phone or a video game.

The traveler walked to the window. The man never looked up. He simply said, "Yep." Assuming he was in the right place, he gave the man a description. Without looking up, the man responded, "We don't have a car fitting that description. It's probably at the other yard."

The traveler sighed and dropped his shoulders. "How far is the other yard from here?"

He told him, "The office is next door."

The traveler didn't say another word. He walked out of the white door and entered the black.

The office was set up similarly. He could easily see the same man sitting at the window, still intently focused on the device. He waited, but received no greeting from anyone. There was a bell on the counter by the window; he rang it and waited for a response.

No one came. He walked back to the first office, and once again the man never looked up. He repeated, "Yep."

"I went next door, and no one came to the window. I rang the bell."

The man responded. "Sounds like a personal problem. I got nothing to do with what goes on over there."

The traveler asked, "May I use your phone to call over there and see if I can get somebody to come to window?"

Without looking up the man said "Nope. That's my competitor. You ain't gone call my competitor from my phone."

In disbelief and confusion, the traveler walked out the door. He stood at the entrance for a moment, not believing what was going on. He took a breath and pulled the door of the black building open to find the man now sitting at the window in front of him.

The man said, "Yep."

The traveler responded in a matter of fact tone, "My car."

The man didn't look up, "What about it? I got several cars." He gave the description of the car, and the man responded, "Yep I got it." He asked how much to get it. The man pulled some paperwork from the box in front of him. He seemed to be reading the paper as he got up and walked back to the window of the other office. He banged on the calculator and scribbled something on the page. He returned to the window and said, "You got the registration for that car?"

The traveler replied frustrated, "No. It's in the car."

The man asked, "Well how do I know it's yours?"

Taking a page from the book of the young lady, he said, "How you know it's not? Have you thought a lot about what you do know and don't know?"

The man bobbed his head in agreement and said "Good point, eighty-five dollars."

He pulled his money from his pocket and slid 5 twenty dollar bills under the window. The man once went over to the first window and used the cash register. He walked back to the window and retrieved the paperwork he initially had. He returned to the other side as he wrote and checked boxes. He made a copy of the document. He then laid both documents on table in the middle of the room. He leaned over the table and scribbled on both sheets. Leaving one sheet on the table, he brought the other to the window. Without looking up, he sat down and passed a ten dollar bill and five ones under the window along with the sheet of paper.

"Take that paper next door and get him to sign it," he instructed.

The traveler looked at him and shook his head.

This was one of the weirdest things he's ever been through.

He took the paper and walked out the door. He entered the other door and found the window empty. He saw the man sitting at the window on the other side. Enraged, he yelled, "Can you come over here and sign this?"

The man shook his head. "That's not my business."

The traveler turned around. He was about to go out the door, but failed to see the point. He turned to the window once more, and the man was sitting in front of him. "Yep," he said.

The traveler took a deep breath and sighed. He passed the slip of paper under the window. The man took the sheet of paper and reviewed it thoroughly. "Did he ask for yer registration? I can't release this vehicle without knowing it's yours."

Since it worked the first time, the traveler asked again, "Well, how do you know it's not mine?"

The man behind the counter replied, "That's why we check registration." He picked up the phone and pressed a single button. After a pause he said,

"Can't release without registration. Well you should have put that on the form."

He hung up the phone. The man said, "Go out the front door, walk passed the office next door and go through the gate. The car is right inside the gate. Get your registration out the car and take it the gentleman next door. The doors are locked, so I hope you got the keys."

Beyond frustrated at the process, he walked out the door, passed the office, and pushed the gate open. His car was sitting a few steps in front of him. He unlocked the passenger side door and sat down to open the glove compartment. He took his registration and insurance forms from the pile and threw the others back into the glove compartment. The insurance dates were valid, but he hadn't paid insurance in two months. As he went to stand, he looked up and was shocked to see identical twins staring at their respective devices, both wearing the same clothes and smoking similar pipes.

He shook his head in amazement. "Oh, for crying out loud."

He walked through the gate, into the black door, and waited. After 3 minutes, one of the men walked into the building.

"I got my registration," the traveler yelled.

"Not my business." The obvious response. Soon, the man walked back out the back of the building. The door opened again. He wasn't falling for the switcheroo, so he just waited until the man came to the window.

"License and Registration?" He retrieved his license from his wallet and grouped it with the papers. The man took the papers, reviewed them quickly, made copies, and returned. "Sorry. He's a stickler for paperwork over there." He slid the bundle of papers, along with a new sheet, back to the traveller.

Without a word, he walked out the door and entered the other building. The man was standing at the window. Neither man said anything. He rang the bell at the counter. "Let me see them papers."

The man went through all the papers reading every single word. He took the new page, stapled it to the first page, and stamped it. He went to the copier, made a copy, and passed the copy to the traveler,

"It's all yours have a nice day."

The traveler asked, "How far is the mechanic from here?"

The man looked up for the first time and responded, "Go out of the front door and go through the black door next to this office." At this point the traveler felt the entire thing had the effect of slapstick comedy.

He went next door and waited. Soon, the man came to the window. "Yep."

The traveler responded, "I need you to take a look at my car."

The man asked, "Will it crank?"

"No."

"Bring it to my shop and I'll look at it."

The close to psychotic traveler said "It's next door! In your yard!"

"It's his shop, not mine. His prices high as a sequoia tree. He'll probably charge $85.00 to tow it over here."

The man walked out the door and slammed it behind him. He stood in front of the building and screamed at the top of his lungs. He opened the door to the black office, where the man stood there with a shocked look on his face. He then opened the door to the white office and met the other man with a similar look. He stood back from the building and yelled, "I have $100.00 cash! My car won't start! I need to leave this yellow brick road to insanity! The first one to work a deal with his brother to fix my car gets my business, and nobody is towing my car anywhere!"

The brothers stood there weighing the options they had before them. The man in the white building said, "That's why your customers come here. You makem' madder than an egg snake that swallowed a white doorknob."

The man in the building in black said, "Well he knows you slower than sap dripping from a maple tree."

Before another word was said. The traveler pointed to the man in the white office and said, "If you don't do it, he's gonna get this one-hundred dollars, and you'll get nothing." He immediately switched hands, pointing at the man in the black office. "If you don't do it, he's gonna get this one-hundred dollars, and you'll get nothing." Pointing at both men he continued, "Or both of you can make fifty dollars. I don't care! I want my car fixed."

The men were obviously perplexed and refused to be out done by the other. They looked at the traveler. The man in the white office said, "Can you give us a minute to confer?" The man walked to the building. He gave the man behind the black door a look of disgust, then slammed door. He did the same to the man in the white office.

He stood outside the building, out of breath from his rampage. His blood was fuming. He was at wit's end and could take no more. It began to rain, and he screamed again. Now thirsty, he realized that he left the 2 liter on the bus. He reached in his inside pocket and grabbed the bag of pizza. He took out a slice and took a big bite, laughing as he opened his mouth to catch rain water. He yelled, "I'm eating and I'm drinking HA!"

After several minutes, the two men opened the gate he entered to get to the car. One of the men said, "You drive a hard bargain but we'll take yer offer." He handed the man the keys, still frustrated, wet, and shaking his head.

The other man said, "Come on in. I guess you can sit in the car until while we look at it."

The traveler jumped in the back passenger seat. The men both got in the car. One man placed the key in the ignition and turned the key. The car did nothing. He looked, grasped the gear shift, and placed the car and park. H turned the key again. The car started right up. Both men turned around and said in unison, "That will be fifty dollars."

The traveler was flabbergasted. He reached in his pocket and placed a one hundred-dollar bill on the armrest. "I don't have change. I'm not getting change. Get out of my car."

The brother on the passenger side looked at his brother and said, "How rude," as they both exited the car.

The traveler angrily screamed "Open the gate." He got in the driver's seat, threw the car in gear, and when the gate opened, he slammed the gas pedal to the floor. Rocks flew as he catapulted out of the gate. He didn't stop or look in either direction. He floored it as he turned onto the highway, finally headed toward his destination.

THE DINER

Though he was out of $100 and had been through one of the most physically demanding ordeals of his life, the traveler had a smile on his face. He adjusted his speed so he wouldn't get a ticket and headed in the direction he had originally intended. After a mile or more, he started looking to see if he saw a small, thin woman with blond hair walking as he drove.

He turned on the radio and began scanning for stations. The radio stopped on a gospel channel, and he quickly pressed the button to continue scanning. Next was a political talk radio show. He pressed the button again. The radio scanned back to the previous gospel station. He pressed the power button.

Once again, he admired the land. He saw neat rows of crops and green grass portioned by fences on both side. Sometimes he would see cows and horses, or a tractor or other farm equipment as it moved along in the fields. But it seemed no one was on the road. He turned on the heat and kept moving. He saw a sign for a diner up ahead and thought it would be a good stop for a bathroom break.

As he approached the diner, there were only 2

cars parked out front: a police car and a 60's model Buick. He pulled between the two cars and jumped out. He walked into the diner, which was surprisingly quite modern when compared to the hotel and the gas station. The counter was lined with brushed aluminum base stools with orange leather upholstered cushions. There were dark tables with 4 upholstered orange chairs surrounding them. Each table had with pea green napkins stuffed inside small juice glasses. The walls were adorned with nostalgic items that worked well in the diner's design. He was impressed. He had expected the greasy spoon image as he approached the diner.

He was greeted by a waitress. She was gorgeous. She appeared to be in her late 20s to early 30s, tall with long locks of brunette hair. She wore a short khaki mini skirt with an orange polo shirt that matched the color of the chairs, and a dark brown apron. She smiled and walked towards him.

"Hey sugar," she said. "Take a seat where ever you like and I'll be over with a menu and water."

He smiled and asked, "Where's your restroom?" She pointed to the corner in the back of the diner. A large, dark brown sign with orange letters reading "RESTROOMS" with a pea green arrow directed him to the facilities. As he walked down

the hallway, there were several pictures of the same diner from different time periods.
He assumed they must have recently remodeled to a trendy look.

The bathroom countertops were granite with different shades of brown and tan. On top of the counters were large, clear basins with ultra-modern, touch less hardware. The cabinets and stalls were all dark woods. There was soap, lotion, hand sanitizers, cotton balls, cotton swabs, paper towels and mouthwash with little cups on the counter. The urinals were touch free with orange deodorizers in the bottom. He approached the stall and did his business. As he stood he read an article that was in front of the urinal.

This diner has been in the same place since 1923. It was a rickety shack for 30 years and known for its pancakes. In 1953, a tornado demolished the towns of Hope, Keep Faith, Believe, and Promise, including the diner. Determine to keep the diner as a staple of the community, the towns of Hope, Keep Faith, Believe, and Promise joined together to rebuild. It has been remodeled every year as each of the towns come together to lend a helping hand to keep this diner a wonderful place for our patrons. We hope you enjoy the food. Don't forget to try the pancakes

He went to the beautiful basin and washed his hands. He dried his hands with a towel and then applied some of the lotion. This was far too elegant to be a diner in the middle of nowhere. He walked out the door and found a seat at the counter on the third stool.

The waitress walked over, sat a menu in front of him, and said, "You gone get a piece of pie on the house. Look at our menu and order whatever you like. We'll have out faster than you can blink. Now what can I get you to drink?"

He smiled, and said,"Coke."

"Coming right up." She brought him a tall original Coca-Cola glass filled to the top and a red and white striped straw.

He looked up and said, "This is really a classy place. I am very impressed with the look inside. Not what I expected."

She smiled and said, "Thank you. I designed the interior myself. I'm happy you like it. I guess I'ma have to make that pie a la mode with such kind words."

He chuckled and took a glance at the menu. They had just about every cuisine you could possibly want: breakfast, burgers, American home cooking, Asian, French, Greek, Italian, Kosher, Mexican, and sushi. His jaw dropped at all the options. He looked up, and the waitress was standing there, still smiling.

"Order whenever you're ready honey."

He said, "I'll have the pancakes."

The waitress's smile vanished. "Do you see pancakes on the menu?" She was right; there were no pancakes on the menu.

"I'm sorry," he said. "I thought you had pancakes. I read the article in the restroom, and it said, 'Don't forget to try the pancakes.'"

She looked out the window, no longer interested in his order. She said, "Well, you gonna order from the menu or the bathroom wall?"

The waitress's attitude barely fazed him, as he was still impressed by the many different choices on the menu. There was Belgian waffles, French toast, crepes, and all sorts of pastries. He had a choice of several meats. The possibilities were endless.

He looked at the waitress and pulled out his card.

"Do you accept this card here?"

She said, "We take payment however you can make it here, sugar."

The traveler ordered a feast fit for a king. "I'll have 3 eggs over easy, waffles, ham, bacon, and sausage. I also want hash browns, with onions and cheese." The waitress continued to stare out the window. She didn't write one item down on her pad.

She smiled and said, "Well that's quite the appetite. You sure you're going to have room for pie a la mode?"

He said, "I'll put the rest of it in the compartment in my wooden leg." It was a term his mother used to use when she would tell her friends about how much he ate. She would say, "I don't know where all of it goes. He must have a wooden leg with a hidden compartment."

The waitress thought about it, and slowly, it made her giggle. "Well that will be right up." she said. She went through the kitchen door, as he sat there sipping cola and smiling as he thought about his mother.

The door opened to the diner, and the little bell

rung on the door above. In walked the police officer from last night. He was followed by another black male, at least 6'3 but skinny as a twig. He had on makeup, blue eye shadow, mascara, and lip gloss. He wore hoop earrings with 3 studs going up each ear. His hair was braided in tiny braids down his back, and he walked in a feminine manner. The two were certainly an odd couple. They went near the middle of the diner and took a seat with their backs to the door. Shortly thereafter, a white male, average build, with brown hair cut into a Mohawk. He had a full sleeve of black and white tattoos on each arm. His ears were pierced with oversized holes. He was intimidating, no question about it.

He walked in, looking suspicious as he surveyed the restaurant. He stopped and stared at the traveler. "Sup?" he said. The traveler nodded, still unsure of who he was or what was his purpose for speaking. The man walked to the table and joined the two men that just walked in.

When he greeted the table, the feminine male jumped up and gave him a kiss as they embraced. The traveler shook his head and turned his attention to the art on the wall. That wasn't his business, and he didn't want to know what was going on.

The waitress flew out the kitchen and went to the table. She hugged every person at the table and began to take their orders. She came back to the drink area and made one cola and a tall root beer float, to which she added two red and white straws. She took them back to the table, placed the float between the lovers, and passed the cola to the officer. As she passed by the traveler going back into the kitchen she said, "Your order is coming up."

The bell rang again as the door to the diner opened. The traveler didn't look at first. He was sure it would be someone more outrageous. The waitress came from the kitchen and greeted the patron. "Welcome. What can I do for ya, sugar?"

The patron said, "I ain't got no money and wanted to know if I could work for some food."

The traveler recognized the voice immediately. He turned to see the woman standing in the front of the diner.

The waitress smiled and said, "Sure sugar. Take and seat and order what you like."

The traveler spoke up. "I'll pay for whatever she wants."

The woman said, "I told you about your generosity, I don't want it!"

The waitress looked at him with shock. "Sugar, you can only pay for yourself here. Nobody pays for nobody. We got a deal, she's gonna work for her meal. You should consider the same. Throwing your card around like its cash. You're gonna pay for anything she wants, Ha!" She rolled her eyes and told the woman to take a seat.

The traveler was embarrassed by the outburst of the waitress. He looked around, and everyone was staring. He turned around and thought to himself about the man who said the people were a bunch of mixed nuts.

The woman came and plopped down on the stool next to him. He looked at her; she had that familiar look on her face squinting as tight as she could.

He leaned toward her and said just above a whisper. "Why did you sit next to me? It's a whole diner full of tables and chairs. If you don't need my generosity, why you feel the need to sit here?"

She turned to him and said, "A fire truck! That is

the dumbest thing I've ever heard. You want to be a fire truck? Do you know I had to walk here with that foolishness on my mind? Who wants to be a thing? You are alive. A fire truck isn't alive. It's man made. It's a tool. I bet you always feel used, well tools are meant to be used. Red and shiny, kept clean. Bathe and put on clean clothes for a change." She shook her head. "I am so mad at you!"

He looked at her and said, "A rodeo clown? Who respects a clown? What do you think that the clowns actually control the bulls? Is that your way of handling the men in your life? Hey, look at me! Then jump in a stack of tires. The bull is looking for the opening in the fence. That's why it keeps spinning around. It's trained to leave the arena after the strap is off of its back; there is no clown escort. How much does a rodeo clown make? No scholarship or Pell grant for rodeo or clown college, so you gave up and now you're mad at the world. Who are you to judge me?"

The waitress, who had overheard the conversation between the two, walked to the obviously disturbed woman and gave her a menu. "Here, sugar. Pick whatever you like, and I'm gonna give you a piece of pie on the house." She cut her eyes at the traveler and said, "A la mode."

The traveler thought of her rant. "Why are you mad at me?"

She took a sip from the glass of water in front of her but never looked up from the menu. "It's not one person on this road, in these towns, anywhere around here, that isn't trying to cope with somethin'. Tryin' to put the pieces of life back together, and here you come completely oblivious. Some people trying to find their place in the world get stuck in these towns. Some just know it's their duty to perform a job. You don't care about life. You act like you're entitled to live, like it's no big deal. I knew you didn't know where you were going."

The officer approached and stood at the counter next to the woman. "You two are like peas in a pod. Neither of you get it, do you? The only difference between you two is that she has an idea of where she's headed and probably remembers why she started traveling. You don't know when you started, or why you started. Neither of you know your destination. Both of you have insulted, disrespected, and disobeyed the laws of this land, and the people in it. These towns have not one person who is a true local. No one was born here. Not one person was raised here. Some people were traveling just like you two, and they can't get past where they are. Some people, like myself, dedicate their lives to making it easy for people to make their travels easier. But everyone is responsible for themselves. First, you need to understand the lay of the land. First town is Hope. It has the largest population. There's green pastures that separate Hope from Hopelessness. Never met anyone that owns the pastures. I don't know where the line of divide lies, or if the pastures are in Hope or Hopelessness.

"Next on up the road is Keep Faith, There are no houses in Keep Faith, only the Motel. Keep Faith is a huge stretch of land with rough terrain and lots of valley and hills. You got Damnation, Redemption and then there's Believe and Promise.

"This young lady was in trouble because she was trespassing. She saw you in the pasture between Hope and Hopelessness. She climbed the fence and was screaming for you to come back. Saw her standing right by the No Trespassing sign. She lost everything she packed for her travel, then she got lost. She tries to help everyone but herself. Just like you, she somehow found her way out of Hopelessness, but many don't. They get distracted by all of the crap and can't find their way back to Hope. Buddy, you said one thing right, IGNORE COW PATTIES. That's the only way to make it from Hopelessness to Hope. But this young lady, she was so worried about you she missed her easy ride to where she was heading.

"The man that insulted you in Hopelessness, along with several of the others you met, choose to be here. They have staked their claims in Hopelessness. I don't patrol Hopelessness. It doesn't need it. They keep themselves in check, because no one aspires to do anything. They're either too lazy to do anything, or they defeat themselves before they get out of bed. Very few people leave Hopelessness once they arrive.

"The man that was heading in the opposite direction calling us a mixed bag of nuts; HA! Trust me, he'll be back. He does this all the time. He makes it just a little bit closer to his destination, and then he turns around to go back to the gas station at Keep Faith. It's the only gas station between the four cities. He can't keep driving, because the he assumes that the only way he will arrive at his destination is to have a full tank of gas when he gets there. How crazy is that? If the tank gets down to 1/4 of a tank, he turns around. I'll let you in on a secret; once you make it to Believe you don't need gas!

"The man who gave you a ride to the gas station—he's a drunk driver. He seriously injured three people and killed one. He lives in Hopelessness. He's one of the ones that sometimes leave Hopelessness. When he does, he continues to drive up and down the road between Hope and Keep Faith, but won't go any further. He is one of the two people that make it out of that town, but they keep returning for some reason.

"I was the best defensive tackle to ever play football in my town. I had more highlights than a rock star's hairstyle. I got a scholarship to go to a division 1 college. I was hit by a drunk driver. The very same drunk driver that I just described. I broke my neck, both legs and was told I'd never play ball again. Instead of making the best of it, I decided to use my size to rob people. I sold drugs, and you didn't mess with me. I was the big man. I got a rap sheet as long as I am tall. I beat up anyone that didn't agree with me, including my wife. One day I came home and she was gone. I ran my son away. And I started my journey. It was long and hard. I thought I was gone die. When I got to my destination, I knew I had to be part of those helping others along their journey. Now I don't have nothing but time on my hands.

"The rich man at the phone booth, he only has faith when it comes to his stocks. He doesn't care about anyone but himself. He makes it to Believe and the credit he lives on sends him back to Keep Faith. He'll never get out of that cycle, because he's a gambler. Some people do it in a casino, others do it with stocks. People like him do it with their livelihoods. He knows he doesn't have the money to support the pricey vet bills. He drove back to Hope, that his stocks will pay off or the dog will recover. His wife is oblivious, never seen her here before, but one thing is certain: she may dodge it now, but someday she's going to have to take the journey. Be happy you're young. It's hard on the elderly. I hate to see the elderly start their journey for the first time because this is a long and hard road.

"The big trucker, he has Cancer. He refuses to heed his doctors' advice on how to treat his issue. He has decided that his faith will cure it. He sits in that truck at the gas station he hasn't left it since he was diagnosed. If he won't do what the doctors say, his faith won't help; it'll make it worse. There is a thin line between faith and arrogance. Same for foolishness.

"Every person that uses that phone booth is looking for a savior. Some act as if they are entitled to salvation. Others have run out of options and salvation is their only hope. Oddly enough, their savior always picks up and listens. It don't mean the savior's gonna change the situation, but they listen. The whole key to it is, faith without work is worthless. The kid that works at the gas station and pizza place also works at the hospital, pharmacy, and a couple other places. He wants to be everyone but himself. He wears those ear buds and listens to music, or he watches TV to learn to mimic others. He refuses to love himself for who he is. One minute he's a rocker, next minute a rapper, then he's straight, next he's gay. He jumps through identities like a chameleon. I'm just waiting. He never stops and never sleeps. I'll find him in one of those pastures one day. I'm willing to bet money on it.

"Both of you heard the woman on dispatch. She never leaves her home, but she knows everybody's business and she tells everybody! She tattle tells so much that no one will talk to her now, except me. She does it because she doesn't want to face her own flaws. She points out everyone else to make herself feel better. It's really tragic; she could be so much more. Imagine if she used her knowledge to patrol, forensics, or in science in some way. I feel for her.

"The man that owns the motel, he is too tight to fix the problems with his very successful business. His greed makes him spend a thousand dollars to save ten. He's stuck in the past. Being the only motel in Keep Faith, he could upgrade that place and charge whatever he likes; where else would people go? He refuses to spend a little money to get a humungous gain. He purposely made sure there are no luxuries—no cell phone signal, no internet. His last upgrade was the bill collectors on the drink machines. Did you see the pool? It has no water, and it's only 3 feet deep. It's a symbol of his shallowness and how cheap he is.

"The housekeeper won't strive to do anything else. She chooses to be a housekeeper. She's a very intelligent woman, but she refuses to learn the language. She knows, 'yes,' 'no,' 'housekeeping,' 'I come back later,' and 'no speak English.' She chose her position because she only wants to make a little money so she can continue her government assistance. She has 5 kids, and they all live in Hopelessness. She leaves from there every morning and goes to Keep Faith to work, and she's teaching her children the same failure when there is a wealth of opportunities out there.

"Oh and you met the brothers. Those two own a gaming company. The two of them are geniuses when it comes to technology. Their yards stretch from Keep Faith deep into Hopelessness. Neither of them want to let the other lead. They have a game release date before Christmas, and they're blowing it! The game won't come out because both of them are arguing about the mechanics of the game work. They will ultimately tank their company because of their competition with one another.

"The husband and wife that gave you a ride, I'm surprised you both escaped them. They are cultist. Now don't get me wrong, I have nothing against religion. Some people need it, some people don't. But no matter your religion, at some point in everyone's life you have to take a journey to find yourself. But those two, they own a compound in Damnation. Many people think they are in Keep Faith, but when you turn and go up that dirt road you find Damnation. It's worse than Hopelessness. Like I told you, some people are here to help others along their journey. Not those two. They are here for their own self-serving desire for followers. They use God as their mask to do their evil. They make people depend on them for their salvation. If you ask me, they probably have good intentions, but their hearts are filled with pride, and they lust for the dependency of their followers. Their greed grows Damnation with every person they pull in. I never seen anybody who went to Damnation leave. They become secretive, and those who were once smiling look solemn. Those who were nervous look scared. The folks stay out in the fields all day long. When they see me approaching, they scatter like roaches in a dark room struck by new light. They got them brainwashed. Their souls are lost. They feed the couple's belief that they can save people. No telling what else they do to them, but I can't do nothing if nothing is reported.

"You think the lady in this diner wanted to be a waitress? She was so talented in interior design, but she was too scared to be what she was meant to be. Nobody could tell her nothing. She didn't want to learn the business, and didn't think of one solitary thing she could learn from going to school or listening to somebody else. She thought she knew it all, and if she didn't know it, it didn't exist. That's why there are no pancakes on the menu; she refuses to learn how to make them. Hopefully one day she'll realize where she is, and this diner will go to the next person. And it will be remodeled by them. I hope it's soon, because I'd love some pancakes instead of these microwave waffles.

"That boy sitting at the table who came in with me all dolled up—he's my son. I spent years of time dedicated to making him the best basketball player he could be. He's had a basketball in his hand since he was a baby. We worked on his jump shot, free throw, and dribbling day in day out because that's what I wanted him to be. I tried to live my dreams through him. He was All State, just like his daddy. He had scholarships and opportunities that many only could dream of. One day he told me he wanted more than anything to be a WOMAN! Then he told me he wanted to be a fashion designer. I disowned him for his choices and lifestyle. He refused to accept that he didn't need my approval to do whatever he wanted to be. I had to grow and learn that he is my child no matter who he wants to be. He gotta understand it's not my approval that he needs he only has to approve of himself.

"His boyfriend is the best tattoo artist in this country. I don't understand why anybody would want to draw on their body or get piercings everywhere. He lives a fast life. He used drugs, pimped hookers, and did everything but take candy from a baby. He may have done that, too. He played the fence dealing with his sexuality. Then one day, I guess he didn't know himself anymore. I found him wondering in the fields, not sure of how to be the person he saw in the mirror.

Both of you have so much potential. You started the walk. You made it through Hope, went to Hopelessness, and came back! It only took both of you one night in Keep Faith. Most people check into that motel for weeks, months, or sometimes years before moving on. You dodged Damnation, and you've made it this far."

He looked at the woman, who sat with her mouth wide open in amazement. Then he looked at the traveler. "Like the lady told you, the two of you are headed to different destinations. Some people want to walk, some want to drive. You decide your own method of transportation. But no one pays for nothing for somebody else here. If you use credit you don't really have, we'll accept it, but you will pay later with a varying interest rate that may be money, but also may be your life. The larger your heart and the greater your deeds, the lower the interest rate. The lady has decided to pay for what she gets with her deeds, and that's totally acceptable. Some people pay cash. But more often than not, people try to get by without paying anything. Usually they end up in Hopelessness, or Damnation, because before you go to Believe or Promise, all your debts must be paid, or you'll be back right here."

The traveler looked at him and took the whole spiel as a load of crap. He smiled and said, "Let me guess. I'm in Penance right now?"

"No, this is Redemption," the officer replied.

The traveler sat back with a hearty laugh, and said, "Sure. Redemption. Where's the choir? Next you'll tell me I'm dead." He looked at the two, the woman and the officer. They looked back at him, and the woman shook her head out of disappointment.

The officer said, "The dead have no need for hope, faith, belief, or promises. They're dead. This is Redemption right here. After you've been redeemed, the possibilities are endless, just like the menu here at the diner. Remember when I gave you your license? That's what this is about. Your identification. The person you see in the mirror. It's not the mirror's ability to reflect that changes; it's the subject of the reflection."

The man looked straight in front of him. Everything made sense, but it was taking time to digest all that he just heard.

The woman asked, "If this is about his identification, then why am I here?"

The officer smiled and said, "You're still focused on everyone but yourself. You don't mind working, you do what you got to do, but you refuse to accept your identity. When are you going to stand up and say, I AM HERE! Your question should have been what about YOUR identity, not how or why are you involved in his. This isn't his personal dream; this is both of your spirits crying for help. You don't have a jacket to protect yourself from the cold. You keep walking, thinking you're helping others when the person who needs the most help is YOU. You have no cash, no checks, no credit, no ID. You have no idea of your actual destination. How did you say it, you'll know it when you get there? This is the first time you've made it to Redemption, and you've been walking between Hope and Keep Faith for as long as I can remember. You're just like the drunk driver, speeding through like a fool. You're always trying to help people—always trying to be a guide from Hopelessness to Hope—when you really only need to worry about yourself."

The man's jaw was dropped. It all made sense. The waitress came out and said, "Sorry it's taking so long. I can bring your eggs if you like." He told her to bring the eggs and cancel the rest of his order. He realized he didn't need everything that he ordered. He worked out an agreement to work off his bill also.

The officer looked at them both and said, "Chew on that for a minute. My coffee's getting cold." Then he returned to his table.

The traveler sat there in dismay. The woman sat next to him, in silence also. The traveler sprung to his feet and walked to the table where the officer sat. He said, "Hello everyone, excuse me for interrupting. How did you know all of that about all of us?"

He smiled and said, "When I ran your license, I got all of your information. The rest I find out from the dispatcher. That's why I talk to her, I guess. I enjoy juicy gossip."

ON THE ROAD AGAIN

The waitress called and said, "Now don't let these eggs get cold. When you finish, I got a crap load of dishes that need to be washed. Little lady, when you finish you can help me do some prep work cutting vegetables."

The woman smiled and politely said, "Yes mam." She still looked surprised from the message she received.

The man sat down and devoured the eggs. He decided to call the loan agency that owned the car. He would tell them to come and get it. He went in the kitchen, which was nothing short of a 5 star gourmet kitchen. The waitress pointed to a sink surrounded by dishes. He didn't mind; he needed time to process the information he received. He washed dishes, finding a peace with every dish, pot, pan, and item of eating and preparation utensil he washed.

The woman received her food, ate, and came into the kitchen. She was given an apron. She cried as she cut onions, green peppers, garlic, and other vegetables. She wondered how long had she been there she had no clue of how long she had been walking back and forth between Hope and Keep Faith. She went to the restroom, and for the first time in a long time, she looked at her reflection in the mirror. She couldn't hold back the tears. She looked at how thin she was. She had cuts and bruises everywhere. She couldn't wait to get to Promise. She knew that she had to make the promise to love and forgive herself. The waitress gave her a bag with a slice of pie. She told her that she didn't think it was smart to pack the ice cream. The woman took the bag, looked back at the restaurant, and walked out the door. The traveler never saw her again.

The traveler worked for the restaurant for several months until he paid his debts. He would sleep in the back, open in the mornings, and close at night. One day he emptied the mop bucket for the last time. He wiped off the counter as neared the exit. He went to shake the waitress hand, and she smiled.

"You better give me a hug. Send me a postcard when you get where you're going."

He smiled and told her, "I will do. Thank you."

As he turned to walk out the door she told him, "Oh yeah, your pie." She held up a bag.

He said, "I thought it was going to be a la mode?

She smiled, and said, "As long as you keep faith and believe that ice cream will still be there and as cold as an Eskimo's pinky toe, the pie will still be hot. I promise."

www.ingramcontent.com/pod-product-compliance
Lightning Source LLC
Chambersburg PA
CBHW071510040426
42444CB00008B/1577